Hollar's England

Overleaf: Osney Abbey, near Oxford. P. 1052

John Aubrey, as an undergraduate at Oxford before the Civil War, had caused drawings to be made of these ruins, believing (correctly) they would soon vanish. He sponsored this plate in Dugdale's *Monasticon*, and commissioned Hollar to etch the ruins from one of the drawings.

Insignes hujusce Fabricæ Ruinas,
quas Antiquitatis ergò plurimum suspexit,
Adolescentulus jamtum Oxoniensib' ascriptus,
&(quod commodum accidit) paulò antequam
Bello Ciuili funditus e medio tollerentur, de-
lineandas curavit, Posteris quasi redivivas
L.D.C.Q.
Iohannes Albericus
de Eston-Pierse
in agro Wilts Arm:
W. Hollar fecit

£10-00

Hollar's England

a mid-seventeenth-century view

Graham Parry

Michael Russell

for Barbara

I am indebted to Gerald Taylor and Michael Vickers of the Ashmolean Museum, Oxford, and to Hugh MacAndrew of the National Gallery of Scotland for their kind help and advice. My thanks are also due to the Master and Fellows of Magdalene College, Cambridge, to the Librarian and Assistant Librarian of the Pepys Library there, to the Librarian of the Royal Library, Windsor, to the staff of the Department of Prints and Drawings at the British Museum, and to the staff of the Print Room at the Guildhall Library; and, not least, to those private collectors who generously made available their prints for reproduction.

University of York, 1980 GRAHAM PARRY

First published in Great Britain 1980
by Michael Russell (Publishing) Ltd.,
The Chantry, Wilton, Salisbury, Wiltshire

ISBN 0 85955 014 1

Set in Monotype Garamond
by Mouldtype Foundry Ltd., Preston, Lancashire
Illustration negatives supplied
by The Scolar Press, Ilkley, West Yorkshire
and Aero Offset Reproductions Ltd., Bournemouth, Dorset
Printed in Great Britain
by Biddles Ltd., Guildford, Surrey
Bound in Great Britain
by The Newdigate Press Ltd., Dorking, Surrey

Contents

List of Plates

The P numbers in this book refer to Parthey's catalogue of Hollar's etchings:
Wenzel Hollar. Beschreibendes Verzeichniss seiner Kupferstiche.

Introduction

THE ENGLAND to which Wenceslaus Hollar came at the end of 1636 must have appeared a tranquil and auspicious place. The Thirty Years' War had desolated Bohemia, his homeland, and brought upon all the participating countries a general decay of fortune which restricted the prospects for an aspiring artist. So when Hollar came to the notice of the Earl of Arundel at Cologne in May 1636, and was immediately taken into his service, he must have felt that he had secured for himself a rather enviable future. Not merely was the Earl a man of high standing in England; he was also a discriminating patron and connoisseur of the arts, whose collection was outmatched only by the King's. He was at present engaged on an embassy from King Charles to the Emperor in an attempt to secure the Protestant succession to Bohemia, a mission which, far from distracting him from his artistic preoccupations, afforded a chance for him to search for talent and works of art the whole length of his travels. He encountered Hollar in Cologne, and on the evidence of his ability engaged him to record the scenes and incidents of their journey to the Emperor in Vienna, and thereafter to return to England in his service as 'caelator' or engraver.

Although the details of Hollar's life are very ill documented, enough remains to trace its main outlines. Up to his meeting with Arundel, his career had not been particularly remarkable. He had been born on 13 July 1607 at Prague, where his father, Jan, was Registrar to the Bohemian Law Court. His mother, who belonged to the minor nobility, died when he was six. According to the inscription on the portrait of him by J. Meyssens, which Hollar etched (P. 1419) and published in Antwerp around 1649, his juvenile inclination was towards miniature painting: 'pr l'art de meniature principalement pour esclairir, mais beaucoup retardé par son père.' His father's objections can only be conjectured, but it is probable that miniature painting, though fashionable, was too dependent on the prosperity of the upper classes to guarantee a sound future. Though he turned to etching as a profession, it is clear that he merely diverted his talents as a miniaturist to another medium, for his accomplished handling of minute detail is undoubtedly one of the great pleasures of his etchings. Engraving or etching would in fact be a somewhat more reliable livelihood than miniature painting, since it could cater to a fairly widespread demand for views, portraits of famous men, scenes of contemporary events, and book illustrations, which were growing in importance.

Prague in the early seventeenth century was a city of fading glories. During the reign of Rudolph II (1552–1612) there had been a flurry of artistic activity, which by Hollar's time had largely died down. Amongst the artists gathered together by Rudolph was Aegidius Sadeler, who had served him as court engraver, and who remained in the city until his death in 1629. Presumably Hollar must have encountered him during his youthful apprenticeship in Prague, for Sadeler was the only engraver of real standing in the city. We know that Hollar left Prague in 1627 and moved to Stuttgart, then to Strassburg, and eventually to Frankfort. It might be that his leaving Bohemia then was connected with the imperial edict of that year banishing all those citizens who would not adhere to Catholicism: it seems likely that Hollar was a person of Protestant sympathies, although his true religious beliefs remain enigmatic.[1] Economic reasons as well as religious pressures could explain his move to Germany at this time.

At Frankfort he joined the workshop of Matthau Merian, a considerable figure in European engraving, and a friend of Jacques Callot. It was here that Hollar probably began to develop his distinctive skills as a topographer, for Merian himself had an admirable manner in this genre, and his workshop produced a large number of German views and cityscapes. Merian's prospects were of great spaciousness, with careful perspectives, yet full of meticulous and apparently accurate detail in the buildings portrayed. He had also developed an effective technique of bird's-eye representation that Hollar was to exploit fully in his own maps and views. In time, Hollar's techniques surpassed Merian's in delicacy of etching, in subtlety of tone and in power of composition, but there can be no doubt that the period spent with Merian did much to establish the nature of his talents, and to refine his style and techniques.

The other formative influence working on Hollar at this early period of his career would seem to be the drawings and engravings of Dürer, several of whose works he copied and etched during the years 1626–49, combining pleasure with publication. The first known plate from Hollar's hand is a copy of Dürer's *The Virgin Embracing the Infant Jesus* (P. 132a), dated 1626. On a portrait of Dürer (P. 1391), he describes him as 'clarissimus pictor, chalcographus, geometer et inventionum picturae pater'. One can see in Hollar's topographical work the qualities he so admired in the German artist: the miniaturist's power of detail, the tranquil atmosphere of undramatic landscapes, the depth and spaciousness of design. In particular, Hollar's watercolour sketches have a distinctly Düreresque quality about them.

After two valuable years spent with Merian, Hollar moved from Frankfort to Cologne about 1633, going northwards, perhaps, to distance himself from the fighting which was growing more intense in central Germany. He now obtained work with Abraham Hogenberg, a successful engraver and publisher, and there he remained for several years, travelling around the Rhineland from time to time to sketch views for his work, and visiting Holland in 1634. So when the Earl of Arundel arrived in Cologne in 1636 Hollar was in possession of a fair body of topographical etchings and drawings with which to impress the Earl and secure a place in his retinue.

This connection with the Earl of Arundel makes the following few years the most clearly defined of Hollar's life. Otherwise, there are few records relating to him, and even fewer letters to him or from him. Most of what we know is based on recollections of his friends, hearsay and rumour, occasional references to him in contemporary letters and books, or

[1] See F. Springell, *Connoisseur and Diplomat* (London, 1963), p. 141 for a discussion of Hollar's religious affiliations. Hind believes Hollar to have been a member of the Utraquists, a moderate Bohemian sect deriving from Jan Hus. Both Evelyn and Aubrey thought him a Catholic in later life. The truth seems quite impenetrable.

conjecture and deductions from his work. But now we can track him in his patron's footsteps, for his travels through Europe with the embassy are copiously illustrated by a remarkably fine and extensive series of drawings, often tinted in delicate watercolours, of which just over a hundred still survive.[2]

The route lay along the plague-stricken and ravaged Rhineland, across southern Germany, through Nürenberg to Linz, where they met the Emperor, Ferdinand II, and began the ultimately unsuccessful negotiations over the future of the Palatinate. Always ready to mix diplomacy with treasure hunting, Arundel made an excursion via Vienna to Prague to view the collections and investigate the art market—for Hollar a last opportunity to see his native city and make a memorial portfolio of sketches that he would etch from time to time for the remainder of his life with the fond nostalgic pleasure of the exile.

Arundel was evidently very satisfied with his new artist, for in May 1636 he wrote in a letter to the Rev. William Petty, his agent in Rome and close confidant in artistic matters, 'I have one Hollarse wth me, whoe drawes and eches Printes in stronge water quickely, and wth a pretty spiritte.'[3] Some degree of good feeling must have existed between them, for we find that while in Regensburg the Earl abetted Hollar's petition for a patent of nobility through his mother's line, which the Emperor appears to have granted more out of respect for Arundel than consideration for Hollar. At any rate, he was now able to style himself Practenberger von Löwengrün und Bareyt, a singularly useless addition as it turned out, though at the time it must have seemed a felicitous prelude to his return to England, where as a titled gentleman he could hope to move easily in the social spheres where commissions might lie thickest.

When he arrived in England, then, in 1636, the prospects facing Hollar were alluring in the extreme: he had a firm post in a peaceable land, under an intelligent and enlightened patron, and he had access to one of the finest art collections of Northern Europe. Thomas Howard, Earl of Arundel (1585–1646), was a fine example of the complete Renaissance man: Earl Marshal of England, skilled in arms; a diplomat, with an international reputation, often the King's proxy; a traveller, multilingual; above all, a patron of the arts and a collector. He had encouraged Inigo Jones, taken him on his travels to Italy, and employed him on his house at Greenwich and at Arundel House in London. He was instrumental in bringing Van Dyck to England; he tried to entice Rubens over; he was patron to Daniel Mytens, the leading painter of James I's reign. His children were tutored by Henry Peacham, the author of *The Compleat Gentleman,* which not unexpectedly was dedicated to Arundel; his librarian was the deep scholar Francis Junius. A man of infinite curiosity, his dominant passion was for antique statuary; his celebrated collection of classical marbles had been purchased, bribed and stolen from Greece and the Levant by his enterprising minions who had ransacked the ancient sites with a mixture of guile and gusto that was typical of the early enthusiasts for the antique. His was the first collection of classical sculpture in England, and marked the beginning of a considerable broadening of taste in this country. His collection of paintings was no less remarkable. According to the inventory of 1655, Arundel had amassed some six hundred paintings, amongst which Titian, Giorgione, Veronese, Tintoretto, Raphael, Dürer, Holbein

[2] See Milos V. Kratochvíl, *Hollar's Journey on the Rhine* (Prague, 1965).
[3] British Museum Add. MSS. 15970 f. 26.

and Van Dyck were impressively represented. Beneath these major collections, there was a descending scale of antique inscriptions, coins, medals, stones, corals and curios, and all the knick-knacks so dear to the heart of the seventeenth-century antiquarian. The fame of these treasures was already widespread, and in particular the details of the marbles and classical inscriptions had been communicated to the world of learning by the scholar John Selden in his *Marmora Arundelliana* (1628).

The Earl was eager to publish descriptions of his masterpieces for the delight and edification of the *cognoscenti*, and to this end Hollar began to produce etchings of selected works for public circulation. In many ways, this process of copying has had more durable results beyond the gratification of intelligent curiosity in the seventeenth century, for a number of subjects have since been lost or destroyed, and only survive to present knowledge in Hollar's etchings.

Hollar lived for the next few years at Arundel House on the Strand, whose rambling precincts are nicely evoked in several etchings. The most attractive feature of the house for the artist must have been its riverside location, providing a fine panorama of the Thames and the crowded buildings on its banks that he was to draw so often, yet with such immediacy. Throughout his life Hollar was entranced by water, and many of his finest compositions are landscapes that incorporate a river or the sea. He loved the long, low horizons that river views entailed, and the harmony of water and sky is one cause of the serenity that pervades much of his work. One suspects that this special sensitivity might first have been induced by a familiarity with Dürer's watercolour landscapes, and strengthened by his extensive travels along the Rhine and residence by the Thames; but whatever its origin, this responsiveness contributed much to his imaginative strength. It was the Thames that provided him with the subject for his first attempt to draw attention to himself as someone other than a copyist of the first order, when he executed the large view of Greenwich (P. 977) in 1637 and dedicated it to Henrietta Maria. It was an arresting début, in the best manner of his continental prospects, combining an airy spaciousness with great felicity of detail. The plate is scrupulously etched to produce those careful gradations of tone that convey the sense of distance so well. The mastery of composition is perhaps best seen in the handling of the vast spaces of foreground and sky in such a way as to give them character and tension, so that they are not just vacancy scarcely veiled, but a natural and satisfying approach to the river at the centre.[4] This print must have served to announce the presence in England of a new and remarkable artist. Indeed, he had no true rivals. In coming to England he was entering a land where the art of etching was barely known, and where there were no established masters.

With his view of Greenwich Hollar began the depiction of the English countryside, towns and monuments that provide us with such an unexampled record of the England of the seventeenth century. There is no systematic intention in his work, except fidelity to his craft, but the cumulative effect of his hundreds of etchings of English scenes fills us with a sense of vicarious participation in the life of the times. Yet what we see is not just a direct transcription

[4] There are three states of this print. The first version carries the dedication to Henrietta Maria, which was later replaced by a set of verses, and there exist also copies in which the shield is left blank. Hind thinks that the reason for the change is the growing unpopularity of the court during 1637–8, so that Hollar or Peter Stent, the publisher, might have felt that the sale of the print would be hampered by its royal dedication.

of the scene, but rather a presentation of what the cultivated seventeenth-century man wished to see. Hollar looks about him with the eye of a gentleman: he sees noble prospects everywhere, stately cities lying by great rivers or in spacious plains. If a lord has built the mansion of his dreams, Hollar will etch it for him, free from the circumambient squalor of the age. The figures who populate these prospects, discoursing with grave faces of *ragion del stato,* or transfixed in eternal gossip, are all of dignified bearing and clad with becoming decency, if not more finely arrayed. Even the ploughmen have a Virgilian poise, and the watermen are worthy of better work. The swarm of people who fill the courtyard of the Royal Exchange (P. 1036) mix business with fine apparel, and there is no doubt that we witness a world of gentlemanly commerce decorously conducted in a palatial setting. Hollar shows us a world where men are proud of their surroundings, admiring of the works of their forefathers and confident of their own dignity and power. It is a world we are familiar with from the complimentary poetry of the age, and could be illustrated with ease from Jonson, or Carew, or Marvell. Indeed, the refined and atmospheric scenes of his patron's seat at Albury in Surrey (P. 954) take us instantly into the world of Cavalier elegance and *élan*; they project the courtly aspirations of a period, and to us they have the nostalgic qualities of an idyll.

Hollar was effectively the first landscapist of note to work in England. The portrait had been the dominant and almost exclusive English form before Hollar's arrival, and such landscapes as there were generally occurred as a rudimentary background for figure painting. A few artists, usually Flemish or Dutch, had made forays into the English scene, such as Antonius van den Wyngaerde, Joris Hoefnagel, or Claude de Jongh, but their occasional compositions were not sufficiently numerous or sustained to create a tradition. There seems moreover to have been little disposition amongst English gentlemen to request landscape compositions. Hollar, however, trained in an important European topographical tradition, and with his long residence in and familiarity with this country, was able to establish the genre and create an enduring taste for landscape here through a long succession of varied prospects in a mature and sensitive style. In the Greenwich plate of 1637, the interest and pleasure lie essentially in the handling of landscape, and the work marks a significant point in the history of English aesthetics. The sheer sustained excellence of his work, coupled with his distinctive delicate manner, provided the basis for a consistent treatment of landscape that was perpetuated to the end of the century by followers such as Francis Place, Francis Barlow, David Loggan, Thomas Johnson, Johannes Kip and Leonard Knyff.

The growing delight in landscape art during the 1630s and '40s is paralleled in poetry by the development of topographical verse; here too there is a similar pattern, as the specific landscape scene enters seventeenth-century verse as the background to such localised poems as Jonson's 'Penshurst' or Carew's country house poems, and later emerges as a subject of primary and independent interest, as in Denham's 'Cooper's Hill' of 1642, from which the Augustan tradition of topographical verse is derived.

Hollar's primacy in English landscape engraving is stressed by John Evelyn, the diarist who in his day was more celebrated as a virtuoso, a man of wide and elaborate learning and varied talents. In his *Sculptura, or The History of Chalcography* (1662), the first book on engraving published in England, he puts forward the hope that 'such as exceed in the talent [engraving] would entertain us with more landskips and views of the environs, approaches, and prospects of our nobly situated metropolis, Greenwich, Windsor, and other parts upon the goodly Thames; and in which (as we said) Mr Hollar has so worthily merited, and other countries abound with, to the immense refreshment of the curious, and honour of the industrious artist' (chapter IV).

Evelyn also conveys some of the pleasure and excitement felt by cultivated amateurs at the reproduction of great works of art, in which Hollar was frequently engaged, and helps us to understand the contemporary feeling about a skill we have ceased to value very highly. 'We do therefore here make it our suite for them [engravers] as what would extreamely gratify the curious, and virtuosi universally, that they would endeavour to publish such excellent things as both his Majesty and divers of the noblesse of the nation have in their possession; and to which there is no ingenious person that will be deny'd access; since if they were well engraven and dispers'd about the world, it would not only exceedingly advance their profit and reputation, but would bring them likewise into a good manner of designing, which is the very life of the art; and render our nation famous abroad, for the many excellent things which it has once again' (chapter IV).

Hollar certainly did much to gratify such expectations, and his first years in England were very fertile in the way of reproductions and views. He also accommodated himself more congenially in his new country by marrying in 1641 a waiting woman of the Countess of Arundel, a Mistress Tracy, of whom a portrait but little other information survives. They had a son ('an ingeniose youth, drew delicately', in John Aubrey's opinion) and a daughter ('one of the greatest Beauties I have seen').[5]

His reception in court circles must have been very cordial, for in about 1640 he was appointed drawing master to the Prince of Wales, the future Charles II. Such an appointment by the most artistically discriminating of English monarchs is a fair measure of Hollar's progress in his first years in this country.

It was natural that Hollar should move into this orbit, for Charles was always anxious to attract artists of talent to his court, and he saw himself in the line of the great prince-patrons of the Renaissance. At this time such talent was invariably foreign: he retained Daniel Mytens from his father's court, Gentileschi and Honthorst came for a while in the 1620s, Rubens was welcomed in 1629–30, and Rubens's outstanding pupil Van Dyck settled in England in 1632. Charles tried hard to persuade Bernini, Velasquez and Rembrandt to add their lustre to his court—without success, however. Mytens had worked originally for Arundel, and had then been patronised by Charles whilst Prince of Wales, and Van Dyck, as we have seen, had come to England under the sponsorship of Arundel before he too was taken up by the King. There were thus some sparkling precedents for a move from Arundel's household into the royal service, so when Hollar was appointed drawing master to Prince Charles it must have seemed as if he was also to be safely established in the royal favour, although as an engraver he could not expect the same rewards as the more esteemed painters.

It is not difficult to understand why the King borrowed Arundel's draughtsman to instruct his heir. Hollar's manner of drawing was at its finest during the 1630s, with an exquisite

[5] O. L. Dick (ed.), *Aubrey's Brief Lives* (London, 1950), p. 163.

delicacy of touch matched with a Flemish precision of detail.[6] His intimate acquaintance with the best masters that came from his close study of the Arundel Collection, as well as his own native freshness of style in drawing, must have recommended him as a mentor for the young prince.[7] Further advancement came around 1640 when he apparently obtained some position in the Duke of York's retinue.[8]

During the years from 1637 to 1644 he must have amassed a fair portfolio of views of the scenes familiar to him. The drawings of the various noble houses that flanked the north bank of the Thames that Pepys acquired for his collection were probably done during this period, as were those evocative scenes of Whitehall and Westminster in all their Gothic dignity. From this time too come those drawings and etchings that preserve the pristine aspect of Inigo Jones's piazza at Covent Garden. Old Lambeth set in its marshes, the Royal Exchange, Lincoln's Inn and numerous riverside scenes were amongst his productions. Much time must have been spent on the elaborate and detailed survey of London from Southwark which was to result in 1647 in the most magnificent view of the city made during the seventeenth century. Outside London his sketches in this period have preserved for us the sight of old Richmond Palace in a number of its aspects, Windsor, Hampton Court, and many of the old castles of the south coast.

Among the curiosities of his work in the 1640s are the sets of seasonal figures that seem particularly dear to Hollar. Instead of the traditional allegorical inventions, Hollar presents us with a series of demure ladies, each in costume appropriate to the season she represents. He evidently held an enduring delight in the varieties and degrees of costume in vogue in the countries he visited, partly no doubt because of the challenge that the various textures of dress had for his etching skills. On another level, however, details of costume appealed to that intense sense of locality that is characteristic of Hollar's best work, and the London backgrounds to several of these seasonal figures (P. 606–8, 610) make a happy combination of two of his favourite genres.

In 1642, however, disaster struck Hollar's domestic economy: Arundel, recognising the danger of civil war, left England for Antwerp. The members of his household were left to fend as best they could, for with the Earl departed, the normal routine of his court collapsed. It might be that figures such as Hollar were still allowed to lodge at Arundel House, but without the financial security that the Earl's presence guaranteed. The result of this disintegration was that Hollar was obliged to become dependent on London publishers, and in particular on Peter Stent. Stent, whose shop was in Giltspur Street, was the most substantial figure in the printselling trade at the time, having taken over the stock of several of his leading predecessors round about 1640. Hollar had already had dealings with him: it was Stent who had published the large Greenwich etching of 1637, for which, according to Vertue, he gave

[6] The drawings he made whilst on Arundel's embassy were the most accomplished of his career, and are usually fully finished. Thereafter his drawings were generally done with a view to later etching, and do not show the same degree of finish.

[7] Vertue records the existence of a small drawing book of Prince Charles with annotations in Hollar's writing then in the possession of the Earl of Oxford, but now unfortunately lost. Vertue recalls that it had sketches of heads and faces, but we have no further evidence of the subjects of Hollar's tuition.

[8] See the inscription on his self-portrait, P. 1419.

the artist thirty shillings. Though this trifling sum seems to have been characteristic of Stent's practice, Hollar nonetheless remained with him, partly because Stent produced very good impressions from the plates, partly because he was the foremost London printseller, and, perhaps most significantly, because Stent was willing to take Hollar on as one of his chief draughtsmen, a gesture that at least provided some assured income, however minimal. He received either fourpence per hour for his work, according to Vertue, or sixpence per print, according to Aubrey, a rather insulting return for one who had been drawing master to the Prince of Wales (a position which had probably lapsed as a result of the political chaos). The situation underlines the familiar tale of the precariousness of an artist's livelihood once his patron failed, and probably also illustrates Hollar's well-known inability to come out on top in any business agreement. The publishers would regard Hollar as a skilled craftsman, to be paid by the hour. Occasionally in his etchings we see his hourglass, sad memorial of his mortality and economic serfdom, through which the pennyworths of his life and art trickled, and which Francis Place, in one of those revealing little details, assures us he was so scrupulous in observing.[9]

It would be appropriate to describe here the method of etching that Hollar exercised. He always etched with acid (*aqua fortis*) as opposed to engraving directly onto the copper plate with needle and burin. There are several accounts extant of his technique, the clearest of which is that given by the antiquarian Richard Symonds in his diary and which was transcribed by George Vertue: 'He uses to buy his water of the Refyners & pay 4*s*. the pound. There is aqua fortis of 8*s*. The printseller at the West end of St. Pauls has brass & copper ready pollished. One Harris a quaker coppersmith & printer uses to sell copper. He lives in a court in Aldersgate Street. 20 February 1649 [1659 ?] I saw Mr Hollar etching & he laid on the water wch cost him 4*s*. pound & was not a quarter of an hour eating. It bubled presently. He stirred it with a feather. He lays on the wax with a clout & smooths it with a feather. He makes a Verge to keep in the water after it is cutt with yellow wax on Tallow melted together & layd it on with a pencil. He always stirrs the aqua with a feather.'[10] Thus the practice would be to rub a very thin coating of a wax compound over the smooth copper plate, and draw the design through the wax onto the plate with a needle, the strength of the stroke naturally conditioning the strength of the line on the plate. A wall of wax and tallow would be built around the plate, and the acid poured in, eating away the copper wherever it had been exposed by the needle. The process is brief, and after the design has bitten into the surface, the plate can be removed and cleaned, and the more delicate areas which are already sufficiently etched can be waxed over, and the plate treated again with acid to deepen the stronger lines. The superiority of the acid-etching method over direct engraving onto the copper plate lies in the greater freedom of drawing that results from not having to cut into the copper, and also in the subtlety of tones that etching allows. Evelyn observed in his *History of Chalcography* that 'aqua fortis gives a tenderness to landskips, trees and buildings superior to that of the burine (tho' that exceed infinitely in

[9] George Vertue, *A Description of the Works of the Ingenious Delineator and Engraver Wenceslaus Hollar* (London, 1745). Francis Place, the Yorkshire artist, knew Hollar well and provided Vertue with much of the biographical material for his book.

[10] Vertue, *op. cit.* (2nd edition, 1759), pp. 133–40.

figures.)'[11] The actual printing of the plate was a function of the printseller, and was executed either by a press or by rollers; it would appear that this printing was a process of some difficulty and skill, to judge by the frequency with which the term 'excudit' or 'excudebat' appears on the prints as a sign of independent expertise.[12]

Though working primarily for Stent, Hollar was still able to work on commission for other publishers, and his much larger output of dated prints in 1643 (about sixty-five, compared with about thirty-five for 1642, and fifteen or so in 1641) shows how he was being forced to live entirely on the proceeds of his work. He published in this year the *Theatrum Mulierum,* an extensive and engaging collection of thirty-six fashion plates of contemporary female costume in various European countries, which now provide us with a great deal of information about the dress of that period. The subject was either extremely popular or close to Hollar's own private pleasures, for the series lengthened over the next few years to one hundred, ranging from the Religious Woman of Antwerp peering out from her tent-like shrouds to the Virginian woman clad only in a loin-cloth. He had previously produced a run of twenty-six fashion plates (on which he had been working since 1635) in 1640, consisting exclusively of English fashions, under the title *Ornatus Muliebris Anglicanus,* showing the range of dress from nobility to countrywoman. Later editions of these show that they were sold by Stent, and it is likely that the *Theatrum Mulierum* series was also marketed through this same channel, though later impressions carry the name of the Antwerp publisher Johann Meyssens, which indicates that Hollar was able to take the plates abroad with him when he left England.

Hollar's sympathies in the Civil War, which was now reaching its peak, were predictably Royalist. When defeat seemed certain, he determined, like so many other Royalists, to quit the country, and sailed to Antwerp. Vertue records a tradition, probably communicated by Francis Place, that Hollar was in the defending garrison at the siege of Basing House in October 1645, when the House was defended by what was virtually a contingent of the Artists' Rifles, including Inigo Jones, Thomas Fuller, William Faithorne the engraver, and Hollar, if we are to believe Vertue.[13] On the other hand there is no contemporary evidence for Hollar's presence, and several of his etchings are dated from Antwerp in 1644, so it seems reasonable to assume that he had extricated himself from the country well before the siege of Basing.[14] Antwerp, where the Earl of Arundel was residing in exile, was the natural refuge, but the Earl had very limited funds and did not in fact employ him. Moreover, Arundel was in ill health, and soon after Hollar's arrival he abandoned the damp climate of Antwerp for Italy, where he died in 1646 at Padua. Hollar resorted to the local publishers, as he had done in London, working particularly for the artist-publisher Johann Meyssens.

During these years in Antwerp, Hollar's output was prolific, as he strove to subsist by copying masterpieces and lesser works, engraving portraits, and illustrating books. He made

[11] Chapter v.

[12] There is only one print on which 'Hollar excudit' appears; this is on the first state of the portrait of Charles II (P. 1442) after Van Dyck, published in Antwerp in 1649.

[13] Vertue, *op. cit.,* p. 142.

[14] Before he left England, Hollar made a singular contribution to the war effort: a set of six very detailed maps of England (P. 652–7) which were made up into a book and advertised as 'Useful for all Commanders for Quartering of Souldiers and all sorts of persons that would be informed where the Armies be; never so commodiously drawne before this 1644. Described by one that travailed throughout the whole Kingdom for its purpose.'

much use of his notebooks and drawings of English views, for he continued to issue copies of works from the Arundel Collection and also quite a few prospects of London and the country scenes he knew. Some of these English views must have appealed to a public that was curious about England because of the Civil War; others must have been aimed at the large community of English expatriates in the Low Countries, but some, such as the six Albury scenes (P. 937–42), must have been the expression of a form of nostalgia, for they cannot have been of great interest to Flemish customers. There seems indeed to have been a deep streak of nostalgia in Hollar that persisted throughout his life: it can be seen in the way he returns time after time to etching the city of Prague, always with delicacy and care, even until the year before his death; it is implicit in the observation he made to Aubrey after his return to England, that 'when he first came into England (which was a serene time of Peace) . . . the people, both poore and rich, did looke cheerfully, but at his returne, he found the Countenances of the people all changed, melancholy, spightfull, as if bewitched.'[15] His later attachment to antiquarians such as Dugdale and Aubrey probably strengthened his temperamental inclination in this direction.

In these years he seems to have set himself the challenge of etching extremely difficult subjects to perfection, as a technical *tour de force* and display of his absolute mastery of his art. Turning aside from the usual landscapes, townscapes and portraits, he executed a series of studies of muffs and shells that are marvels of delicacy and fineness. He had obviously felt the challenge of the fur muff whilst working on his fashion plates in England, for there these pieces of winter apparel are always treated with great attention and skill. He began a series of individual studies whilst in England in 1642, and continued them until about 1647, and each plate is admirable both as a still life and as a consummately fine rendering of texture. Equally, the studies of shells are attractive both as compositions and as examples of the subtlety that etching can achieve in the capturing of tones and contours. Like the muffs, they are virtuoso pieces, and mark the high point of technical powers. It has frequently been remarked that Rembrandt's etching of a shell (c. 1655) is very likely a tribute to and emulation of Hollar's artistry in these designs; they are certainly worthy of such admiration.

In 1646 he published a remarkable series of etchings of insects, based on specimens in the Arundel Collection. Whether Arundel had assembled his Cabinet of Insects because they appealed to his sense of the curious or the grotesque, or because he had an embryonic interest in entomology, is difficult to decide; yet Hollar's rendering of these beetles, butterflies and moths observed their fanciful shapes with a scrupulous accuracy that was not surpassed until Robert Hooke published his microscope studies of insects in *Micrographia* (1665). The publication and success of Hollar's studies of insects and shells reveal a developing public interest in the minutiae of natural history, and these essays in scientific observation also help to explain why he was welcomed and patronised by members of the Royal Society in the 1660s.

The most impressive plate, however, from an English point of view, that came from Hollar's hand in his Antwerp years is the magnificent and vast View of London (P. 1014) by which he is chiefly known in this country. The great panorama of the city was perhaps inspired by Visscher's similar view of 1616, but Hollar's is more detailed, accurate and spacious, and achieves the artistic feat of presenting all London as a visible community lying by the Thames. It remains the most complete and fascinating delineation of old London before the Fire.

[15] Dick, *op. cit.*, p. 163.

Another significant work from the Antwerp period is the self-portrait that he etched from Meyssens's painting for inclusion in the collection called *Images d'Hommes d'Esprit Sublime* (1649), a title which must surely have gratified this generally unassuming artist who so often found himself humbly petitioning for employment. We see him sitting with the instruments of his craft before him, holding a copper plate of the St. Catherine (P. 177) attributed to Raphael, which was in the Arundel Collection but is now lost. Presumably it was as a copyist that he was best known to his public, or at least it must have been the role in which he desired to be known. To be an imitator of great models in those days was a creditable occupation, with even some of the lustre of original creation. To be a fine copyist meant, after all, that one was master of many styles. It is especially felicitous that Hollar should have chosen to display such a plate as the St. Catherine, for the very fact of its disappearance indicates how valuable are Hollar's records for the connoisseur and art historian. The brief *curriculum vitae* that accompanies this portrait is virtually the only biographical detail that we have more or less directly from Hollar. Hind has translated it as 'Gentleman, born at Prague in 1607: was by nature strongly inclined to miniature painting, chiefly in colouring prints, but discouraged by his father, left Prague in 1627, lived in various parts of Germany, and devoted himself to the practice of engraving; left Cologne for Vienna with the Earl of Arundel, and returned via Prague to England: there he entered the household service of the Duke of York but returned on account of the war to Antwerp where he still resides.'[16]

Hollar stayed in Antwerp for about seven years, though towards the end of that period he appears to have made contact with the exiled English court in France. In 1650–1 we find dated prints of Jersey, at a time when the Duke of York was there. By the end of 1651, to judge by a dated plate of St. Paul's, Hollar was back in London. It would seem that the much-reputed antiquarian William Dugdale was the moving force behind his return, for Dugdale was contemplating the publication of several large works which needed illustration by an accurate and sensitive hand. Hollar with his long experience was a natural choice. Soon after his arrival, Hollar was arrested on some unknown suspicion, perhaps as a spy, perhaps for contravening some religious edict, possibly because of his recent association with the royal court abroad; at any rate the incident passed off without repercussions, and Hollar was not molested again during the rest of his life in England.[17]

Dugdale would appear to have been Hollar's steadiest patron after his return, providing him with a series of important commissions that involved the cutting of some 302 plates for him over the years up to 1673. The most numerous collection amongst these belongs to *The Antiquities of Warwickshire* (1656), that meticulous model of local history where nearly two hundred of his engravings appear.[18] Even though nearly half this number are simply coats of arms for the display of Warwickshire heraldry, the enormous amount of work involved in

[16] A. M. Hind, 'Wenceslaus Hollar', in *Connoisseur,* October 1933, pp. 215–27.

[17] See the letter in the British Museum, Add. MSS. 21450. f. 1, undated and unaddressed, though it is probably to Dugdale, in which he complains of his arrest.

[18] Anthony Wood's comment in his diary conveys the profound pleasure that this work had for its audience. 'This summer came to Oxon *The Antiquities of Warwickshire* written by William Dugdale, and adorn'd with many cuts. This being accounted the best book of its kind that hitherto was made extant, my pen cannot enough describe how A. Wood's tender affections and insatiable desire of knowledge were ravish'd and melted down by the reading of that book.'

the volume means that Hollar must have been extremely busy preparing these plates for some considerable time prior to its publication. Dugdale was an honest and substantial gentleman, careful in his accounts and prompt in his payments; in fact, precisely the sort of patron that Hollar stood in need of, with his apparent lack of financial acumen. Moreover, Dugdale paid generously for his work, having a thorough appreciation of his artist's talent, so that we hear of Hollar receiving up to five pounds per plate (generally five pounds for the full page ones). Dugdale's interest must have guaranteed Hollar a fair competence over the years.[19]

Books like the *Monasticon Anglicanum* and *The History of St. Paul's Cathedral* seem to have been brought out on a semi-subscription basis, with wellwishers and local worthies contributing to the cost of plates of some private interest to themselves. This helped defray the heavy charges that Dugdale incurred in producing these large tomes, and occasionally when such sympathisers wrote to Dugdale about the inclusion of some favoured scene, they would request him to have Hollar execute it — shadowy intimations of the regard in which the engraver was held amongst the cultivated classes. Thus Sir Edward Walker, K.G., an early reader of the first volume of the *Monasticon,* having discovered a connection between his family and the Abbey of Burton, desires to commemorate the venerable association, and writes to Dugdale from his exile in Amsterdam: 'The consideration whereof (in despite of the low and despised condition I am reduced unto) induceth me to have the thought to give a Print of the Remaines of that Abby and Church, if there be any to be inserted in ye Worke. Therefore, if it bee to be donne lett me speedily know, and I will employ my old friend Mr Hollart to do it, and send a Draught of my Armes with an Inscription to be added to it.'[20]

Again, the Rev. Thomas Barlow, contributing a plate to *St. Paul's* writes: 'I receaved your's wherein you tell me the Plate will stand me in I shall not question the price, soe it be well done. I know Mr Hollar is an excellent person, and well deserves all incouragement, nor shall I be wanteinge, or unwilling to pay him liberally for his labour; onely you be the Judge, and what you say, I will send.'[21]

The History of St. Paul's Cathedral is an outstanding piece of antiquarian research, a work of industry and sustained enquiry into rolls and records that evolved into a lucid exposition of the cathedral's growth and development, as well as providing a superb *catalogue raisonné* of its contents. Hollar's etchings for the book have the same quality of fidelity to the fact and reverence for the idea of history that Dugdale communicates so well. The combination of accuracy and the invariable neatness of design, as well as the atmospheric charm of the interiors, place these illustrations among the most evocative of the architectural prints of the seventeenth century. The subsequent destruction of St. Paul's in the Great Fire has made Hollar the sole

[19] See Horace Walpole, *Anecdotes of Painting in England, with additions by the Rev. James Dallaway* (London, 1876), volume III, p. 166. Hollar received £185 10*s*. 0*d*. for the forty-five plates he did for *St. Paul's*. Dallaway also states that it was Dugdale who wanted Hollar back to England to prepare the plates for the *Monasticon*. (See pp. 163–75.)

[20] 6 August 1655 in W. Hamper, *Life, Diary and Correspondence of Sir William Dugdale* (London, 1827). The plate was not in fact etched until 1661.

[21] *Ibid.,* 26 September 1656. Hamper's *Life* contains many details of the payments made to Hollar, as well as lists of the subscribers to plates which Hollar cut. *Inter alia,* we learn that unused copper plates cost 4*s*. 6*d*. Something of Dugdale's affection for the artist emerges from such an entry in his diary as that for December 1661: 'Payd for a Gown cloth, wh. I sent to Mr Hollar, 20*s*. For making it, 4*s*. 6*d*.'

preserver of its ancient fabric, for Dugdale himself made no attempt to present the visual aspect of the church in his description. For those who now gaze at the forlorn charred stumps of Elizabethan effigies in the crypt of Wren's church that are all that remain of the old St. Paul's, these engravings serve to depict something of the Gothic grandeur of the original, and the magnificence of its monuments.

Admirable and historically invaluable as these plates are, however, they are not without their shortcomings. When compared to the London scenes of the 1640s, such as the views of the Westminster area (P. 1037–40), they reveal the growth of a certain frigidity of line and atmosphere. The indefinable sense of presence that permeates his earlier work has evaporated. The same strictures may be made against many of his etchings for the *Monasticon:* they are masterly architectural designs, but the warmth and delicacy of line that filled his earlier views are no longer as noticeable. One of the reasons for the decline in atmospheric pressure, as it were, may be the absence of human figures from these designs; without them, Hollar cannot convey the feeling of these buildings belonging to and forming the background of a society. Unique and fascinating they often are, but some of them approach the fascination of the museum piece, devoid of an affecting humanity. From Hollar's point of view, there was the disadvantage that for the *Monasticon* he had often to work from designs submitted to him, and therefore lacked the vital knowledge of the way a building was united with its environment. Furthermore, Hollar's finest work is usually related to his talent as a miniaturist, and often in the etchings for Dugdale the folio-sized plates are too large for an optimum approach to the subject; also, when he was working from submitted designs, there was probably inadequate detail shown on them, and he would be reluctant to improvise decoration in illustrations to books dedicated to historical accuracy—hence the occasional vacancy of some of these productions.[22]

Notwithstanding these aesthetic deficiencies, both *St. Paul's* and the *Monasticon* are triumphs of the preservationist spirit of the antiquarians. Men like Dugdale, Dodsworth, Evelyn, Ashmole, Browne and Aubrey were activated by a natural delight and curiosity in their historical antecedents; but what gave cogency to their enquiries and precipitated an unprecedented antiquarian activity were the depredations of the Puritans after their seizure of power in the 1640s. Their zealous destruction of anything smacking of popery—and after all, virtually all the contents of an Anglican church had such a taint—made it extremely clear that a whole world of antiquity was on the edge of extinction. The ruthless modernism of the Puritans stimulated a powerful literary counter-reaction, for even if the Puritans could not be prevented from defacing monuments and smashing stained glass, mementoes could be made and oblivion thwarted by intelligent records. Apart from the deliberate spoliation of churches by the men of plain religion, the incidental furies of the Civil Wars had caused much additional damage, particularly in the ripping up of church brasses and lead roofs for use in the manufacture of armaments. By the 1650s there was a great deal of mouldering ecclesiastical architecture in England that had been in good condition under Charles I. The quartering of troops in cathedrals, churches and Royalist mansions had not improved the interiors of those places. St. Paul's itself had been used for the stalling of the horses of the London militia during the time that

[22] In the engravings of the monuments in St. Paul's it is likely that Hollar worked partly from drawings provided by William Sedgwick, who had originally aided Dugdale with his research in the 1640s.

Dugdale was making his observations. Inigo Jones's Corinthian portico, built at Charles's own expense, was let out for shops, and badly hacked about as a result. In January 1653, according to a contemporary record, 'A part of St. Paul's fell down'. It was unlikely to be restored under the Commonwealth, and who knew when the Commonwealth might end? Outside the capital, the castles of the country were being pulled down in Cromwell's policy of defortification. When to all this was added the memory of the havoc caused by the dissolution of the monasteries a century before, and when one viewed the scarce-remaining heaps of stone into which so many of those vast edifices had dwindled in three generations, one understood how greatly the ancient land was changing. The realisation of how much could be lost in so short a time provided a powerful incentive to those who cared for their past, and who recognised how inadequately it was recorded. Hollar, with his accuracy, his lifelong involvement with the art of sensitive recording, and his association with connoisseurs and amateurs, was a natural ally of the preservationists, and the body of his etchings have made him one of the chief restorers of the world we have lost.[23]

The *Monasticon Anglicanum,* begun by Dugdale and Dodsworth, and carried on alone by the former after Dodsworth died in 1654, is one of the greatest undertakings of seventeenth-century scholarship, and it dragged its enormous length through the presses for eighteen years. This vast compilation of all the histories of all the monastic foundations in England and Wales, with all its elaborate documentation and description, remains unrivalled, and is still an indispensable source for information concerning the monasteries. The three folio volumes came out in 1655, 1661 and 1673, with Hollar contributing fifty-six illustrations to the whole. The rest of the prints were mainly carried out by D. King and R. Hall, whose productions only serve to emphasise the superiority of Hollar's work, and to point out how dismal was the state of architectural engraving amongst English artists. The awkwardness, the heavy line drawing, the insensitivity to subtlety of light, add up to a general inelegance. Amongst Hollar's representations, those of Lincoln, York and Canterbury are outstanding in their compositional power. They convey a strong impression of having been done *in situ,* whereas others, such as Winchester, have a quality of isolation about them that suggests they were done from drawings supplied by other artists.[24] As a whole, however, there is no doubt that Hollar's work in the *Monasticon* constitutes the finest description of our major churches and cathedrals in the seventeenth century. His best designs set standards of truth and beauty that were not approached again until the nineteenth century, and in the quality of their etching they remain unrivalled.

[23] John Aubrey, the archetypal reader of books such as *St. Paul's,* well expresses the gratitude with which they were received, and dreams of bringing out a similar book himself, to be called *Draughts of the Seetes and Prospects.* 'If these views were well donn, they would make a glorious volume by itselfe, and like enough it might take well in the world. It were an inconsiderable expence to those persons of qualitie, and it would remain to posterity when their families are gonn and their buildings ruined by time or fire, as we have seen with that stupendous fabric of Paul's Church, not a stone left on stone, and lives now only in Mr Hollar's Etchings in Sir William Dugdale's History of St. Paul's. I am not displeased with this thought as a desideratum but I do never expect to see it donn; so few men have the heart to do public good to give 4 or 5 pounds for a copper plate.' (Quoted in Anthony Powell, *John Aubrey and His Friends* (London, 1948), p. 273.) Aubrey lived up to his own standards by contributing to the third volume of the *Monasticon* a plate of Osney Abbey (P. 1052), copied from a drawing he had presciently commissioned when he realised that the abbey might be knocked down.

[24] Dugdale's diary (Hamper, *op. cit.*) confirmed that this was often the case. E.g., '1 June 1665: Payd Mr Hollar for etching 3 more plates. (Delivered to Mr Hollar 7 draughts more.)' Designers who supplied Hollar with sketches included Richard Newcourt, Thomas Johnson, Edward Mascall and Richard Hall.

Work for the untiring Dugdale forced Hollar to defer for a while a request for illustrations from another ardent conservationist, his friend John Tradescant the younger. The elder Tradescant, the erudite gardener whose passion had been the introduction of rare and exotic plants into England, had enlarged his love of collecting beyond mere horticultural limits and had built up an extremely varied holding of rarities and curiosities that had some claim to be the first museum in England. Besides a large natural history collection, Tradescant had gathered stores of minerals and fossils, a miscellaneous assortment of antiquities, and much material that would now be considered ethnological: implements, craftwork and clothes from the New World and from the East. There was also, inevitably, a small admixture of the fabulous and odd (a roc's claw, some phoenix feathers and the like), but altogether it was a very impressive and intelligently grouped collection that could be of much value in the advancement of learning. Indeed, the Tradescant Collection later formed the major part of the new Ashmolean Museum at Oxford, after Elias Ashmole had deviously acquired possession of it and presented it to the University. The younger Tradescant had continued to extend his father's collections, and wished to provide a catalogue of them for the use of the learned world; for illustrations worthy of this project he chose Hollar, and according to the preface of the book he was willing to delay the printing of *Musaeum Tradescantianum* for nearly a year, until 1656, so that Hollar could be free to prepare the plates. Once again, in this commission we sense the esteem in which Hollar was held by his contemporaries for work that combined a high level of scientific accuracy with accomplished artistry.

In 1660 came the Restoration, from which Hollar must have expected to benefit, for his connections with the court dated way back to the pre-Revolutionary years. Had he not been drawing master to the new King, and a member of his brother the Duke of York's household? Had not his loyalist inclinations been quite evident in his actions and choice of companions? A place, a pension, some royal act of favour or commission would seem a possibility.[25] Yet so it seemed to a host of other deserving men, and Hollar received no tokens of recognition, very probably because he lacked the friendship of some well-placed nobleman who might direct royal attention towards him. The main effect of the Restoration on his career was rather ironic, in that the author and publisher John Ogilby had the neglected Hollar cut the plates for his opportune souvenir programme, *The Entertainment of His Most Excellent Majestie Charles II in His Passage . . . through London to His Coronation,* a folio panegyric published in 1661. The long rows of the King's procession that fill the plates might be of interest to students of precedence in the seventeenth century, and have also a certain sartorial interest, but on the whole they give the impression of being rapidly executed.

Hollar's connection with Ogilby dated back at least to 1654, when he provided the majority of the plates for Ogilby's fine edition of Virgil, published in that year. The illustrations are done in the fashionable baroque manner of the time, a style that Hollar tended to adopt for the illustration of classical texts. Ogilby was a versatile literary entrepreneur who gratified the desire for curious and topical information of his contemporaries as well as their aesthetic sensibilities, with a number of sumptuously produced books, to which Hollar frequently

[25] Likewise, later on he might have expected some advancement from Prince Rupert, who was keenly interested in engraving, and who introduced the technique of mezzotint into England. Hollar had done two portraits of him (P. 1315 and 1499) and cut a print to celebrate his naval victories over the Dutch (P. 1246).

contributed the large copper-cuts. Their collaboration continued with *The Ephesian Matron* (1666), *An Embassy from the East India Company to the Grand Tartar Cham, Emperor of China* (1669), which Ogilby translated from the Dutch of John Nieuhoff, *Africa* (1670) and *Britannia* (1675).

Hollar also resumed relations with the publisher Peter Stent after the Restoration, providing for him initially a portrait of Charles II's bride Catherine of Braganza (P. 1448) in 1661, then various drawings of animals and flowers, as well as a book of designs that Hollar had compiled to teach figure drawing. Curiously, Stent refused to take the etching of Hobbes (P. 1417) that Hollar submitted for publication, though the grounds of his refusal are not known. Stent died in the Plague, and most of his stock seems to have been taken over by John Overton, who became one of the most influential London publishers for the next forty years. Overton also took over as an employer of Hollar, and according to Vertue 'kept him in his House, confined to Hard Labour, and small pay, at his usual method, by the hour glass'.[26]

The Great Plague of 1665 hit Hollar hard: his only son died, the 'ingeniose youth [who] drew delicately', who probably was being trained by his father. (It is not known when Hollar's first wife died, although recent investigation has established that his second marriage, to Honor Roberts, took place in 1656 at the church of St. Giles-in-the-Fields.) The Plague affected both life and livelihood: amongst the booksellers and those associated with them, trade virtually ceased as the more prosperous part of the population left the metropolis for the shelter of the country. The pestilence lingered on into the next summer, when it was succeeded by the Fire, and in this catastrophe the booksellers were amongst the chief sufferers. At the onset of the fire, the city stationers, all clustered around St. Paul's Churchyard, had moved their stocks into the church of St. Faith's, in the crypt of St. Paul's, as the safest place imaginable to them. Faith was not enough, however, for the church was incinerated on the fourth of September. 'The ruines of the vaulted roofe falling broke into St. Faith's which being filled with the magazines of bookes belonging to the Stationers, and carried thither for safety, they were all consum'd burning for a weeke following.'[27] Not just the books, but the prints and copperplates of the stationers would also have been deposited in that church, so the loss to the trade must have been almost inestimable. Although the rest of the city's commerce soon recovered, the book trade had almost ceased to exist. Evelyn wrote later in the month: 'Onely the poore Booke-Sellers have ben indede ill-treated by Vulcan; so many noble impressions consum'd by their trusting them to the churches, as the loss is estimated neere two hundred thousand pounds: which will be an extraordinary detriment to the whole Republiq of Learning.'[28]

[26] *Walpole Society Publications,* volume I, p. 34 ('Vertue Notebooks').
[27] John Evelyn, *Diary,* 7 September 1666.
[28] Letter to Sir Samuel Tuke, 27 September 1666. See also 'Rege Sincera', *Observations both Historical and Moral upon the Burning of London, September 1666* (London, 1667, reprinted in *Harleian Miscellany,* volume III, p. 282). 'As for Books, the Booksellers, who dwelled for the most part round about the Cathedral Church of St. Paul, had sheltered their Books in a subterreal Church under the Cathedral, called St Faith's, which was propped up with so strong an Arch and massy Pillars, that it seemed impossible the Fire could do any harm to it, but the Fire having crept into it through the windows, it seized upon the Pews, and did so try to examine the Arch and Pillars, by sucking the moisture of the Mortar that bound the Stones together, that it was calcined into Sand: so that, when the top of the Cathedral fell upon it, it beat it flat, and set all things in an irremediable Flame. I have heard judicious Men of that Trade affirm, that the only loss of Books in that place, and Stationers' Hall, Publick Libraries, and private Houses, could amount to no less than 150,000 Pounds.'

The loss of so much labour and stock must have meant hard times for most connected with the world of books, but Hollar's way of profiting from the disaster was by exploiting its sensational topicality. With a provident sense of occasion, he made his way to his favourite vantage point at St. Mary's, Southwark, and recorded the scenes of desolation and holocaust on the far bank. These views (P. 1015, P. 1003/4/6, P. 1028) are amongst the most memorable and evocative that he ever produced, showing the full extent of the fire across a great waste of ruin filled with the shells of churches, the effect of the desolation being intensified by the long panoramic shape of the etchings. St. Paul's is always the focal point of these scenes, and the most affecting, no longer the measure of the city's pride, but a mark of its downfall. Hollar's use of an earlier drawing of London in its prosperity in P. 1015 makes a particularly poignant contrast with the same scene in ruins. Seeing the two views side by side, one begins to appreciate the impact of the countless sermons preached at the time on the theme of the fire as a judgment of God on a city corrupt in luxury and pride. One also feels the force of Evelyn's brief comment, 'I went again to the ruines, for it was now no longer a citty.'[29]

One result of the Fire for Hollar was his involvement as cartographer in the designs for the rebuilding of London. He had been working on a map of the city before the Fire, and events now turned this into a fortunate circumstance for him, as he was able to cooperate with those who were preparing plans for the new city. For projecting the reconstruction of such a large area, some accurate map was essential; and Hollar was in a position to supply it. Evelyn talks of the difficulty of planning without adequate topographical information in a letter to the Secretary of the Royal Society in which he is discussing his submission of his architectural ideas to the King: 'The want of a more exact plot, wherein I might have marked what the Fire hath spared, and accommodated my designe to the remaining parts, made me take it as a *rasa tabula,* and to forme mine idea thereof accordingly: I have since lighted upon Mr Hollar's late Plan, which looking upon as the most accurate hitherto extant, has caused me something to alter what I had so crudely don.'[30] This presumably refers to P. 1003, the same print that Pepys admired: 'My Lord Brouncker did show me Hollar's new print of the City, with a pretty representation of that part which is burnt, very fine indeed, and tells me that he was yesterday sworn the King's Servant, and the King hath commanded him to go on with his great map of the City,[31] which he was upon before the City was burned, like Gambout of Paris, which I am glad of.'[32] It seems likely that this was the occasion when Hollar was awarded the handsome title of Scenographer Royal by the King. Charles, however, was not prepared to finance the position, but instead addressed an appeal to the Lord Mayor of London recommending Hollar's cartographical work and requesting subscriptions for its completion.

It was in his official capacity as Scenographer Royal that Hollar made his last extensive journey, when he was sent by the King with the surveying party to Tangier in 1668. Tangier had been brought as dowry to Charles by Catherine of Braganza, although it was a rather specious offering, since the territory was not really in Portugal's free gift, its control being contested by the local Moors. Nevertheless, an expedition sailed under Lord Henry Howard,

[29] *Diary,* 10 September 1666.

[30] Letter to Oldenburg, 22 December 1666.

[31] This is either P. 1002, an unfinished map of London, or more probably P. 1007, a very large map on twenty plates, finally published in 1677.

[32] H. Wheatley (ed.), *The Diary of Samuel Pepys* (London, 1928), vol. VI, p. 72. (Entry, 22 November 1666.)

Arundel's grandson, to chart this theoretical extension of British power, managing to remain there over a year, during which Hollar did a fine series of drawings and etchings of the port, its approaches and defences. On the return voyage his ship, the *Mary Rose,* was intercepted by Turkish ships, and only the navigational skill of the captain preserved Hollar from death or the slave trade. He promptly turned the situation to his advantage by etching his impression of the encounter and persuading Ogilby to insert it into his volume *Africa* (P. 1247).[33]

On his return, he must have resumed working for Dugdale and the various London stationers with whom he had connections. Around this time he must also have been busy cutting the last plates for that solemn and definitive work of Dugdale's fellow antiquarian, Elias Ashmole, *The Institution, Laws and Ceremonies of the Most Noble Order of the Garter.* This long maturing design finally emerged from the press in 1672, but its inception dated as far back as 1655, when Ashmole feared that the Order might perish under Republicanism, so he undertook it, as he says in the preface, 'in case the Eclipse, it then waded under in our Horizon, should prove of so long Continuance, as that many occurrences, worthy of knowledge, might come to be in a manner forgotten.' Hence Ashmole indefatigably compiled its history, ceremonies, rites, and their significance, yet over such a period of time that what began as an act of preservation ended as a celebration of new growth, and the final plates show the feast of the Order in full Restoration splendour. Hollar's first known association with this enterprise can be traced to 1659, when Ashmole recorded in his diary for 25 May: 'I went to Windsor and tooke Mr Hollar with me to take views of the Castle, etc.'[34] The result of these visits is a large number of extremely fine prospects of the Castle and studies of St. George's Chapel, for the illustrations of the finished book are essentially a magnificent record of the home of the Order.[35] Amongst the most outstanding of these etchings is the aerial view of Windsor (P. 1072) with its imaginative approach and masterly handling of perspective. The grasp of the whole complex of buildings is quite remarkable. The whole sequence of scenes from varied viewpoints makes up a comprehensive picture of mid-seventeenth-century Windsor, particularly if to these we add the large plate (P. 658) from Ashmole's posthumous *Antiquities of Berkshire* (1719), and the earlier small view, P. 914.

During his last years, Hollar continued in the well-established patterns of his life, providing the stationers and publishers of London with their requirements: maps, the occasional news item, and, most notably, title pages, for in this field he was one of the most sought after engravers in the country, because of the strength of his compositional power, and the assuredness of his designs.[36] His last large-scale commission was the etching of Robert Thoroton's *Antiquities of Nottinghamshire* (1677), a handsomely produced volume characteristic of the

[33] His reward for a year's surveying service is variously reported as £50 and £100.

[34] C. H. Josten (ed.), *Elias Ashmole* (Oxford, 1966). Diary, 25 May 1659. Amongst Ashmole's papers in his museum are four drawings, probably by Hollar, of Windsor (MSS. Ash. 1131 ff. 179, 180) but not used in the *Book of the Garter* or otherwise engraved.

[35] It may be that Ashmole initially feared that Windsor Castle might be pulled down by the Protector, in keeping with the general practice of defortification.

There is a letter in Ashmole's papers from Sir Thomas Herbert, dated 31 March 1680, thanking him for the gift of the *Garter* book: 'I put a high value upon it both for ye matter stile and method, as also for ye variety of uncomparable Sculptures. Mr Hollars death is much lamented. They are a great Ornament to your labour.'

[36] See Appendix for list of books published in England containing frontispieces and etchings by Hollar.

vogue for county histories at that time. These surveys always gave an opportunity to display the most important towns and venerable churches; nor did they fail to present in great detail the seats of the nobility and their graves and memorials. Since the gentry of the region were likely to be the main supporters and purchasers of such ventures, their interests invariably feature prominently. It would appear that Hollar was unable to accompany Thoroton on his perambulation of the shire (as he had done with Dugdale in Warwickshire), since the plates are etched after designs by Richard Hall. Hollar was probably unfit for travel in 1676 and did the work at home from the supplied drawings. There are many scenes of great charm amongst these illustrations, but the larger ones tend to suffer from Hall's rather bleak delineation of architectural detail.

The final major work of Hollar's to be published in his lifetime was, rather appropriately, funereal: the elegiac series of tombs in Francis Sandford's *Genealogical History of the Kings of England*. Most of these studies of noble monuments and scutcheons date back to 1665–6, but Sandford was not in a position to publish until 1677. There are some superb specimens amongst these illustrations, notably P. 2282, Edward IV's tomb at Windsor, where the light is particularly harmonious and evocative.[37]

Hollar died on 25 March 1677, and, as he had resided for some time in Gardiner's Lane, Westminster, was buried in the parish church of St. Margaret's, where in the register he is described as 'The Famous' although no monument was raised to him.[38] No monument, no funeral verse in an age that was profuse in its obsequies, no expressions of regret in the letters or diaries of his friends; he died quite unregarded. This is all the more curious when one considers the circle of his friends and acquaintances, for they included many of the eminent intellectual figures of the time, several of them—Evelyn, Ashmole, Aubrey, Wren, Hooke—members of the new Royal Society. (Indeed, he etched the frontispiece to the official *History of the Royal Society,* by Thomas Sprat (1667), a symbolic action in some ways and suggestive of his relation to the Society.) His standing with these men, however, is rather puzzling. He flits in and out of the diaries and letters of the period, frequently praised for his 'admirable and ingeniose inventions', yet rarely appreciated personally. Many speak of him as 'my good friend, Mr Hollar', yet he evidently lacked interest as a personality in an age so prolific in memorable men. The lack of anecdotes about him in Aubrey's 'Life', the only contemporary attempt to provide something more than a brief factual account of his career, is symptomatic. We are forced to the sad conclusion that his contemporaries simply did not find him very interesting, although they well appreciated his talents as an etcher. All we catch of his personality is Aubrey's observation, 'He was a very friendly good-natured man as could be, but Shiftlesse to the World, and dyed not rich.'[39] He was above all a useful man. Moving as he did amongst antiquarians, collectors and projectors, most of them industrious publishers, he was always available to embellish their works and to provide accurate and superbly executed illustrations for books whose authors prided themselves on the accuracy of their information.

[37] Parthey believes this to be Hollar's last plate, though it is difficult to see on what grounds he holds this opinion. It is probable that it belongs with the majority of designs to 1665–6.

[38] The epitaph in St. Margaret's was put there by George Vertue in the eighteenth century. Ashmole was the only person known to have noted Hollar's death in his diary.

[39] Dick, *op. cit.,* p. 163.

Hollar's greatest admirer amongst his contemporaries was John Evelyn, who, being a connoisseur of engraving, appreciated his genius as an artist and not, as most others tended to do, just as an illustrator.[40] In his already mentioned *History of Chalcography*, published in 1662 and presented to the Royal Society, Hollar figures as the leading exponent of engraving then working in England, and Evelyn had backed his judgment by making an extensive collection of his prints, as did his friend Pepys.[41] In his biography, Aubrey, who also thought that Hollar 'hath donne the most in that way that ever any one did', evidently regards Evelyn as the main source of detailed information on the engraver. They were friends of long standing, and must have first met through the Earl of Arundel as early as 1641.[42] When Evelyn came to launch his verse translation of Lucretius in 1656, it was Hollar whom he had engrave the frontispiece after a design by his wife Mary Evelyn. It was the versatile Evelyn, too, who designed the title page for the *History of the Royal Society*.

In many ways Evelyn is an ideal specimen of the audience for which Hollar worked: wealthy, cultivated and intelligently curious; a passionate lover of antiquities, both domestic and foreign; a great reader and admirer of fine books, as ready to enjoy a sumptuously illustrated translation of the classics as to wonder at the Great Wall of China in one of Ogilby's encyclopaedic books. He was an ardent connoisseur of painting, having seen many of the masterpieces of Europe in his travels, and he held that the next best thing to having a gallery of masterpieces oneself was to possess them in reproduction. He was fascinated by great men, collecting the portraits of the outstanding men of the age in large numbers; the very wealthy, like Clarendon, might make such a collection in oil paintings, but Evelyn was typical of his class in acquiring engravings of the figures who made history. He bought prints of notable events as a record of the remarkable times in which he lived. His collection had, as he frequently observed, the Horatian virtue of delighting and instructing, for he felt that his prints were of great use in the education of a gentleman. Evelyn regarded Hollar as an artist who contributed a great deal to the advancement of knowledge in his time, a disseminator of intelligence, a man who furthered understanding of the visible world, whilst being a supreme master of one

[40] Evelyn's essay on engraving remains very helpful in conveying something of the esteem with which the art was regarded by the cultivated. Even if we grant that it is a panegyric on a favourite topic of Evelyn's, and prefaced by many approving citations from classical authorities to prove its antique dignity, it draws attention to the considerable following the art had amongst modern nobility, instancing Louis XIV, Prince Rupert and the Earl of Sandwich. Engraving, we learn, is undoubtedly a challenge worthy of the noblest spirits: 'There never was any famous in it but who was by birth or education a gentleman.' He observes how useful the medium is for spreading information widely, and also considers it a desirable form of national propaganda, advertising the art treasures in the country's possession and displaying the splendour and dignity of the towns and buildings. Much of the essay consists of a rather tedious parade of names of engravers with their chief works, but to a later age the intervening sentiments are of much greater interest than the facts that Evelyn supplies.

[41] Pepys also gathered together a fair collection of Hollar's drawings, which he probably had direct from the artist. They are now in the Pepys Library at Magdalene College, Cambridge, along with his collection of engravings.

[42] There is a sketchbook of Hollar's in the John Rylands Library at Manchester which may once have belonged to Evelyn, for it bears his signature 'Johannes Evelynus' and the inscription 'Ce que j'ai jay receivé. Vigilantia cum diligentia 1641.' Their first meeting may have been on 29 June 1641, when Evelyn went to Arundel House to sit for his portrait to Vanderborcht, a painter who had entered the Earl's service at the same time as Hollar, during the mission of 1636. Hollar is mentioned for the first time in the Diary under that date: 'My very good friend, perverted at last by the Jesuits at Antwerp to change his religion; a very honest, well-meaning, simple man.'

of the fine arts. Thus, writing in praise of him, and after complimenting him on his Arundelian successes, and his etchings after the great masters, he lists his other accomplishments: 'books of Landskips, Townes, Solemnities, Histories, Heads, Beasts, Fouls, Insects, Vessels, and other signal pieces . . . with other innumerable frontispieces, and things by him published and done after the life, and to be (*eo nomine*) more valued and esteemed than where there has been more curiosity about Chimaeras and things which are not in nature; so that of Mr Hollar's works we may justly pronounce, there is not a more useful and instructive collection to be made.'

These observations by his friend express some of the ways in which Hollar served his time. Aubrey looked at him with a narrower interest, as a preserver of vanishing scenes, as an artist whose copperplates had some power against the erosions of time, and it is this attitude which is likely to prove most sympathetic to the modern viewer. An exclamation typical of Aubrey follows upon his discovery of some of Inigo Jones's drawings 'of the old Gothick, or ancient Castles' which were sadly deteriorating: 'I have often intimated to some of our Gravers to make them publick: but I cannot perswade them to it. But had the ingeniose Mr Wenceslaus Hollar lived, he would have donne it, upon my request. Of these once stately Castles, there is not now a stone left upon a stone.'[43]

Since Aubrey's time many more stones have been irreparably displaced, but our visual knowledge of seventeenth-century England remains quite extensive, and for much of this knowledge we are indebted to the varied work of the 'ingeniose Mr. Hollar'.

[43] Dick, *op. cit.,* Introduction, p. xcix.

[from] Wenceslaus Hollar: self-portrait. P. 1420.

1. Albury Manor, Surrey. P. 954.

The halcyon mood of pre-Civil War England is superbly caught in this scene of rural elegance. Throughout the 1630s the Court and its attendant literary and artistic circles sustained the myth of peaceful, prosperous England under the benevolent care of the King, preserved from the ravages of the wars that convulsed Europe. Rubens painted *The Blessing of Peace* for Charles I as his contribution to the myth; the Cavalier poets celebrated their fortune at living in a golden age. Richard Fanshawe's lines are characteristic of the euphoric complacency of the Court:

White Peace (the beautiful'st of things)
Seems here her everlasting rest
To fix, and spreads her downy wings
  Over the nest.

As when great Jove usurping reigne
From the plagu'd world did her exile,
And ty'd her with a golden chaine
  To one blest isle:

Which in a sea of plenty swamme
And turtles sang on ev'ry bowgh,
A safe retreat to all that came
  As ours is now.

Albury was a late medieval manor house acquired by Hollar's patron, the Earl of Arundel, in 1637. The house was burnt down at the beginning of the eighteenth century.

The composition of this work seems indebted to Joris Hoefnagel's 1582 view of Nonsuch Palace – the animated arrival of a coaching party through the woods is a motif Hollar probably borrowed from Hoefnagel and improved by integrating it so naturally into the scene.

1A. Detail from 1 (enlarged 100%).

2. Equestrian portrait of the Earl of Arundel, 1639. P. 1352.

3 and 4. Arundel House. P. 1034 and P. 1035.

Arundel House, the London residence of the Earls of Arundel on the Strand, was originally the town house of the Bishops of Bath, who were deprived of it in the reign of Edward VI. The house appears to have been a conglomeration of buildings from late medieval and Tudor times. It was here that Hollar lived from his arrival in England in 1636 until his patron retired to the Continent in 1642, and one of his most considerable tasks at this period was to record the superb collection of paintings and statuary that Arundel kept there. During the Commonwealth the house was confiscated and used for entertaining state visitors, but was returned to the Howard family at the Restoration. Thomas's grandson, Henry Howard, the house's new owner, was encouraged by Evelyn to bestow the remaining family treasures on the world of learning, with the result that he presented the collection of marbles to the University of Oxford, and the library to the Royal Society, which held its early meetings in Arundel House. The mansion was eventually demolished in the 1680s.

These two prints were among the many that Hollar etched after he had moved to Antwerp, following his patron into exile. Although the subscription states that Adam Bierling drew the scenes and Hollar etched them, the manner is entirely Hollar's. P. 1035 (no. 4), *'meridiem versus'*, is in fact looking north. The church tower visible over the roofs is St. Clement's, to the north-east of Arundel House. Conversely, in P. 1034 the countryside in the distance lies to the south of the Thames. There is also a drawing of Arundel House in the Pepys Library Collection at Magdalene College, Cambridge.

In the top print a departure seems imminent. The large coach to the right was the family's travelling coach for longer journeys, similar to the one seen arriving at Albury (no. 1). The small variety, for town use, can be seen in the left-hand corner of the other view.

In the lower print (*'meridiem versus'*) the building on the right with the very large square window in the roof was probably Hollar's drawing room, amply illuminated for his miniaturist's work. By the door there appear to be two paintings propped against the wall, presumably pictures from Arundel's collection that have been brought for copying.

5. The Tower of London. P. 908.

Fortress, prison and armoury, the Tower stood over London as a protection and a threat. So enduring did it seem that popular tradition ascribed its foundation to Julius Caesar and believed it was coeval with British history. The Tower was also at this time the repository of the Crown Jewels and the State Archives, and contained the Mint and the Royal Menagerie.

The number of wherries on the river remind one that the Thames was the main thoroughfare of London for centuries, for transport by water was invariably faster than progress through the crowded and poorly maintained streets. Along the wharf are rows of cannon, presumably disused.

6. London from the roof of Arundel House. P. 1011.

A fine small view, dating from Hollar's first years in England, showing the dominating bulk of St. Paul's. The gabled building beyond the parapet on the left is part of the Inner Temple. Across Old London Bridge to the extreme right lies St. Mary Overy's.

7 (below). St. Mary Overy's, Southwark. P. 910 (reduced 20%).

The curious name of this church is perhaps derived from the Anglo-Saxon *ofer* (genitive *ofres*), a bank, thus meaning St. Mary's of the Bank, or Bankside. The church, now Southwark Cathedral, was originally part of an Augustinian priory, and became the parish church of Bankside at the Reformation under the name of St. Saviour's. As such it was the local church for the nearby playhouse, and a number of figures connected with the Elizabethan theatre are buried there, including the playwrights Fletcher and Massinger, Shakespeare's actor brother Edmund, and the manager of the Globe Theatre, Philip Henslowe, whose diary is so valuable a source of theatrical information. Chaucer's contemporary, the poet John Gower, is buried there, as is the sombre Jacobean divine Lancelot Andrewes.

Hollar made a larger but coarser etching of St. Mary's for the *Monasticon*. This print is dated 1647.

8. Greenwich (two plates). P. 977 (reduced 45%); with (right) 8A, Greenwich, right hand plate, second state (reduced 45%).

Published in 1637, shortly after Hollar came to England, this etching combines delicacy of line with mastery of the topographical landscape. Certainly this work set new standards in the art of landscape in England.

The Tudor building on the left was a royal lodge, later rebuilt for the astronomer Flamstead and established as the Royal Observatory. In the middle distance stands the Queen's House, Inigo Jones's first major architectural venture, commissioned under the patronage of Anne of Denmark and erected during the years 1616–35 (and so only just completed at the time of Hollar's view). The two figures that give interest to the foreground yet direct the attention to the prospect are another manifestation of the delight that Hollar took in costume studies. The pair are dressed for the summer, with the lady on the right wearing a mask to protect herself against the sun – though the clouds (right) in the second working of this print seem certain to take care of that. In this second state the dedication is deleted, to be interpreted as a sign of the growing unpopularity of the monarchy in the late 1630s.

The conception of landscape evident in this etching is derived from Matthau Merian, who had taught Hollar in Frankfort, but here are qualities that enable Hollar to surpass his former master. It represents, too, the extension into England of an artistic convention well established in the Low Countries: the combination of a topographical landscape with costume studies. Its origins go back to a series of engravings showing the major cities of the world, the *Civitates Orbis Terrarum*, published by G. Braun and F. Hogenberg in Antwerp and Cologne from 1572 onwards. Amongst these views are a number of plates by the Antwerp engraver Joris Hoefnagel, presenting long prospects of a town in a landscape, with the foreground occupied by figures displaying the costume of the locality. The engravings of Hoefnagel continued in extensive circulation into the seventeenth century (the sixth volume of the *Civitates* came out in 1618) and Hollar was evidently acquainted with his work, for it exercised a definite influence over the composition of his own early landscape productions.

9. Richmond Palace. P. 1058 (reduced 30%); with 9A, detail (enlarged 25%).

This imposing Tudor palace was built by Henry VII between 1497 and 1501 after fire had destroyed its predecessor. Henry VIII permitted Cardinal Wolsey to use it after Wolsey had been persuaded to give Hampton Court to the Crown. As one of a network of royal palaces around London, it was a popular residence for important members of the royal family. Prince Henry, the elder son of James I, a talented and intelligent youth who died amidst universal lamentation in 1612 at the age of eighteen, lived here with his brother Charles for most of 1604–12. Charles, after his accession, gave the Palace and Manor of Richmond to his Queen, Henrietta Maria. The building was much misused during the Commonwealth, and although it was returned to Henrietta Maria in 1660, it never flourished again, and was demolished in 1703.

In some copies of this plate (of 1638) it is possible to distinguish the Prince of Wales's feathers on the roof of the covered boat by the bank; thus it has been suggested that the group in the foreground shows Charles the Prince of Wales on the extreme right, his brother James, Duke of York, next to him, wearing a hat, while the little girl could well be the Princess Mary. The courtiers have evidently doffed their hats in the presence of royalty.

The sight of a fairly large ship by the palace reminds us how far the Thames was navigable in the seventeenth century. The curious contrivance on the wharf on the extreme left of the scene is a wooden crane for unloading ships.

10. Hull. P. 984 (enlarged 10%).

The fortified town is now so rare in England that this print is a striking reminder of the formidable appearance that many English towns retained in Hollar's lifetime. As an important seaport Hull was especially well defended, as much against Scottish armies as against naval attack. In 1640 the town had been put in a state of readiness for Charles I's war against the Scots, but Hull turned against the royal cause. Charles, needing a strong port for his northern campaign, besieged the town twice in 1642, without success. On the second occasion the defence was maintained by Lord Fairfax. This print was probably issued in 1642, when Hull was at the centre of public interest.

The fortifications, dating from the fourteenth century and strengthened by Henry VIII, decayed and were demolished towards the end of the eighteenth century.

Hull was represented in Parliament by the poet Andrew Marvell from 1659 to 1678.

THE TOWNE OF HVLL
KYNGESTON VPON
HVLL
This Humbre is broad against this Towne, 2 miles or better
THE RIVER
HVMBER
RIVER
HVLL
A. the olde ferye place
B. Salters staires
C Hornesey staires
D Chapell staires
E Bishops staires
F Scalelane staires
G Kings staires
H heringe staires
I Horse staires
K Bruer lane
L the bocherie
M Finkell streete
N Ogger lane
Fruite market
Whitmeat Market
Corne market
The Rope rie
Whitfrier lane
Scole lane
Beverly gate
Easte
Southe
Weste
North
Hollar. fecit
English miles
Easte
the NORTH SEA
PART OF NORFOLK
The Spurn head
Flamborough head
Brydlington
PART OF
Hull
YORKE
SHIRE
LYNCOLNE
SHIRE
Lyncolne
Yorke
PART
OF NOTTIN
GAM
SHIRE
Nottingham
Weste

11. Large map of England, with royal medallions. P. 651 (reduced $17\frac{1}{2}\%$).

It is unusual for maps to be produced by the process of etching, for they do not generally need the wide range of tones that etching can provide; the simpler method of engraving is usually preferred. This map is based on Saxton. A later edition exists with the head of Charles II included.

A Catalogue of all the Shires, Cities, Market Townes, Castles Parishes, Rivers, Chases, Forrests & Parkes in all England and Wales,

Shires	Cities	Mar: Townes	Castles	Parishes	Riv:	Chas:	For:	Parkes
Barkeshire	0	11	2	140	3	0	1	13
Surrie	0	7	0	140	1	0	0	17
Bedfordshire	0	10	0	116	1	0	0	12
Buckingham shire	0	11	0	185	2	0	0	15
Cambridge shire	0	6	0	163	1	0	2	5
Cheshire	1	9	3	68	9	0	0	18
Cornwall	0	23	6	161	7	0	3	9
Cumberland	0	8	5	58	20	0	1	84
Darby shire	0	8	4	106	15	0	0	35
Devonshire	1	40	5	394	5	0	2	22
Dorsetshire	0	18	6	248	4	1	0	11
Durham	0	5	4	62	11	0	1	26
Essex	1	21	1	415	7	0	2	19
Glocestershire	1	20	1	180	12	1	4	2
Hampshire	1	18	5	248	4	0	0	23
Hartfordshire	0	18	0	120	1	0	2	25
Herefordshire	0	8	7	176	15	1	1	8
Huntingtonshire	0	5	1	78	1	1	0	73
Kent	2	17	8	398	6	0	1	20
Lancashire	1	8	6	36	33	0	2	33
Lecestershire	1	11	2	200	1	0	0	12
Lincolneshire	1	26	2	630	9	0	0	1
Middlesex	2	3	0	75	1	1	0	4
Northampton shire	1	11	2	326	5	0	3	4
Nottingham shire	1	11	0	168	5	0	1	8
Northumberland	0	11	12	40	21	0	1	8
Norfolke	1	26	0	660	3	0	0	0
Oxfordshire	1	10	0	208	3	0	4	9
Rutland	0	2	0	47	0	0	0	4
Shropshire	1	13	15	170	18	0	7	27
Somersetshire	3	29	1	385	9	0	2	18
Staffordshire	1	12	5	130	13	1	1	38
Suffolke	0	28	1	464	2	0	0	25
Sussex	1	18	1	312	2	0	4	33
Warwickshire	1	12	1	158	7	1	0	16
Westmoreland	1	4	6	26	6	0	2	19
Wiltshire	1	21	1	304	5	1	9	19
Worcester shire	1	7	3	152	5	1	2	16
Yorkshire	1	46	15	563	30	4	8	72
Anglesey	0	3	0	83	8	0	0	0
Brecknokshire	0	3	4	70	25	0	0	2
Cardigan shire	0	4	6	77	26	0	1	0
Carmanthinshire	0	6	4	81	20	0	1	2
Carnarvan	0	5	3	75	17	0	0	0
Denbighshire	0	3	3	53	24	0	0	0
Flintshire	0	3	4	24	4	0	0	2
Glamorgan shire	0	7	12	151	16	0	0	5
Montgomery shire	0	5	3	42	28	0	0	1
Monmouth shire	0	6	7	142	15	1	0	8
Merioneth shire	0	3	2	34	26	0	0	0
Penbroke shire	0	6	5	142	6	0	2	5
Radnor shire	0	4	5	43	13	0	0	0

12–17. By Albury. P. 937–42.

After his removal to Antwerp Hollar produced this group of six scenes (dated 1645) set around Albury, the Earl of Arundel's country seat in Surrey. There was always a strong element of nostalgia in the artist's temperament, so these scenes of rural tranquillity in England may well have been an antidote to the anxieties of his uncertain position as a refugee on the Continent. They must also have been intended as a consolation to the ailing Earl, who wrote to Evelyn in 1646 about his deep feeling for Albury 'where I hope to be ere long, and end my dayes there'.

bey Albury

bey Alburye in Surrey
W. Hollar fecit 1645

bey Albury

18. Westminster Hall and New Palace Yard.
P. 1040 (enlarged 10%).

Westminster Hall is the most important structure remaining from the old Westminster Palace, which was the principal residence of the English Kings until it burned down early in the reign of Henry VIII. The building dates back to the very end of the fourteenth century, and as well as being the royal banqueting hall until superseded by Inigo Jones's hall, it was for centuries the home of the various Courts of Law. The notorious Star Chamber, which was suppressed by the Long Parliament in 1641, was located here, Charles I was tried and condemned here, and a few years later a reversal of fortune saw Oliver Cromwell's head impaled and displayed on the front of the Hall, along with the skulls of the regicides Ireton and Bradshaw. In the seventeenth century, incongruous amongst the Law Courts, there were stalls selling books, toys and trinkets in the Hall.

The clock tower on the right is a work of Edward I's reign. The ancestor of Big Ben, its vast bell named Great Tom could be heard as far away as the City on calm days. 'By this tower standeth a fountain, which at coronations and great triumphs is made to run with wine out of divers spouts' (Stow).

Beyond the fountain is the great gatehouse begun by Richard III in 1484, known as 'the high tower of Westminster', or Highgate. It was taken down in 1706. New Palace Yard itself was swept away in 1865 in the replanning of Westminster which accompanied the rebuilding of the Houses of Parliament.

The description of the scene as 'Westminster haall' suggests that the print (dated 1647) was published in Antwerp.

19. Westminster. P. 1037.

Parliament House, on the left of this print (of 1647), was originally St. Stephen's Chapel, built in the mid-fourteenth century by Edward III to replace a foundation of King Stephen's. At the Dissolution it was given over to secular purposes and served as the House of Commons until it was destroyed in the calamitous fire of 1834. Its relatively small size enables one to understand how easily the Gunpowder Plot might have succeeded.

In front of the Abbey's north transept stands the ancient bell tower, and on its right the tower of St. Margaret's, the church where Hollar is buried.

The landing stage gave access to New Palace Yard (see no. 18).

est-monastery, vulgo. Westminster haall

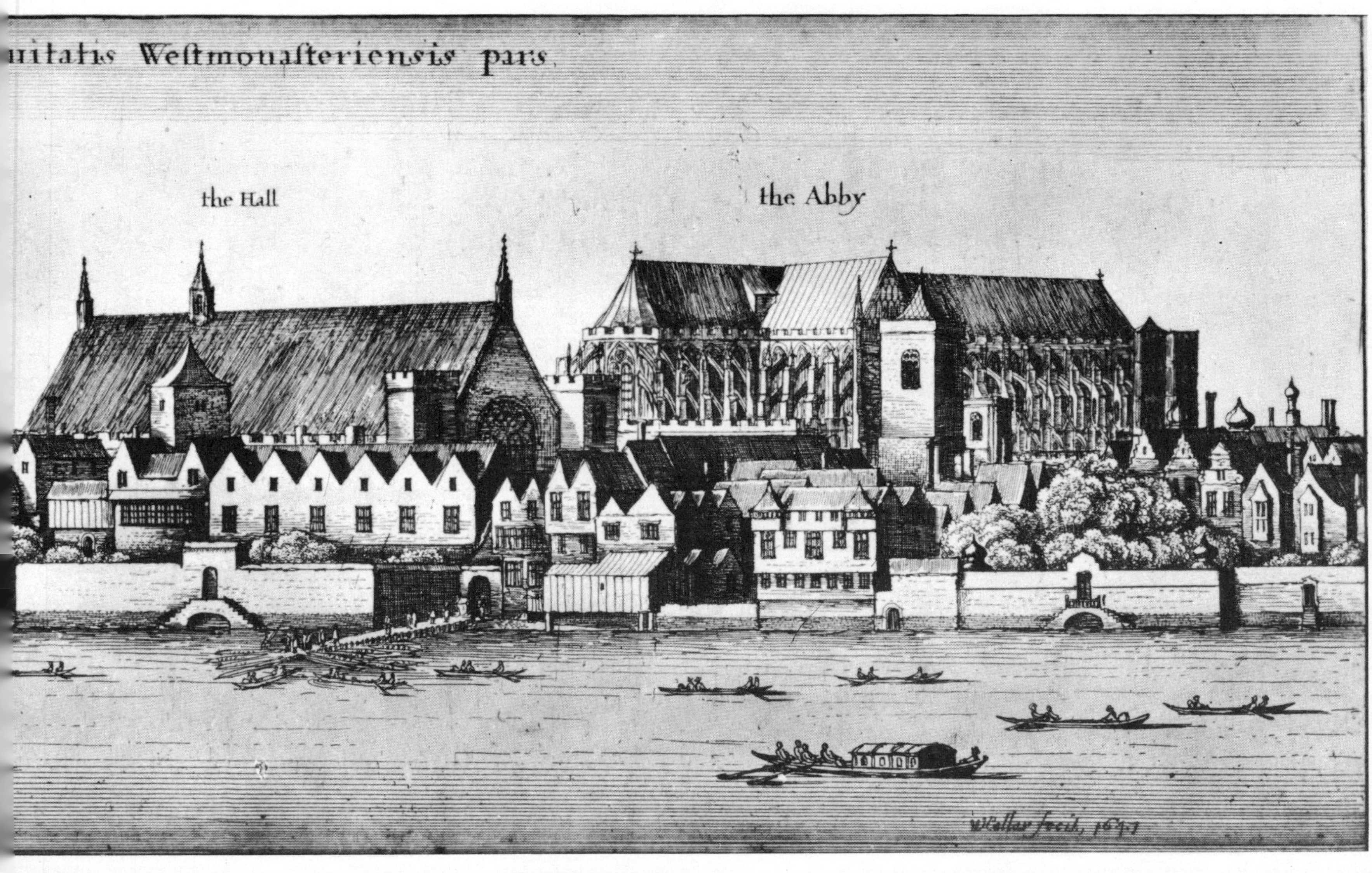
uitatis Westmonasteriensis pars
the Hall
the Abby

20. Lambeth House. P. 1038 (reduced 10%).

Lambeth House was then as now the London residence of the Archbishops of Canterbury. A largely Tudor assemblage of buildings, it was conveniently situated, in the days when the river was the main road of London, close to the Houses of Parliament and Whitehall. Hollar's view, published in 1647 when he had moved to Antwerp, was made shortly before the old Hall was destroyed during the Commonwealth. The sheds overhanging the river on the right are presumably privies.

21. Whitehall. P. 1039 (reduced 10%).

Whitehall was originally York House, belonging to the Archbishopric of York, but it was acquired from Wolsey, who was Archbishop of York among his many titles, by that even more successful collector of palaces, Henry VIII, and thereafter became the main royal palace in London. A large complex of buildings mostly Tudor in period, it extended from the Thames to St. James's Park, and from Scotland Yard up to Westminster. Under both James I and Charles I, extravagant and grandiose schemes of rebuilding were contemplated; Inigo Jones supplied James with a plan for a vast classical palace, on a scale similar to the Louvre, but the perennial Stuart impecuniosity delayed the scheme until the Civil Wars rendered it redundant. Only Jones's design for the Banqueting House was carried out, after the old building was burnt in 1619. This hall, seen in the centre of the view, was the first thoroughly Renaissance building in England when it was completed in 1622, and with it Jones established his ascendancy in architecture and the triumph of the classical style. Rubens painted the ceilings in 1635. This hall, built purposely for banquets, revelry and masques, was ironically the scene of the Stuart tragedy, for from one of its upper windows in 1649 Charles I stepped out on to the scaffold.

Whitehall was eventually destroyed by fire in 1697, and with the accession of Queen Anne the palace of St. James's became the royal residence.

22. London from near Arundel House. P. 911.

A view of London taken from a point just east of Arundel House. Undated, but the costume of the couple on the landing stage suggests the 1640s.

23. Lambeth from Whitehall. P. 912.

The buildings on the right formed part of the riverside range of Whitehall Palace. The projecting structure with stairs was the watergate that gave eminent visitors direct access to the Palace; lesser men used the wharf.

24. Tothill Fields. P. 913.

Tothill or Toothill Fields lay between Pimlico and the Thames. In the seventeenth century the area was a place of recreation for the citizens, and was used for the military exercises of the trained bands, for archery, and occasionally for duels. (Pepys records an assignation here, far from his usual haunts.) A notable feature of the Fields was a maze, presumably represented by the bushes in the centre of this view.

25. Portrait of John Milton. P. 1679.

If the date of 1637 is correct, this is an unusually early portrait, for Milton was then still a comparatively obscure figure. However, *Comus* was published in that year, and this etching may have been prepared for inclusion in the book, though not used.

26. Wenceslaus Hollar, after Meyssens. P. 1419.

This etching, after Meyssens, with whom Hollar was friendly in Antwerp, was included in the series called *Images d'Hommes d'Esprit Sublime* (1649), a collection of portraits of leading practitioners of the arts. Hollar holds a copper-plate of St. Catherine, one of the patron saints of learning and the arts. The original painting, attributed to Raphael, was in the Arundel Collection but is now lost; Hollar, however, had made an etching of it (P. 177), so it is a happy coincidence that permits him to appear both as artist and preservationist. Beside him lie his etching tools and acid. The view through the window is of Prague, with the Cathedral and St. George's Church, and behind the artist hangs his coat of arms, reminder of his noble origins in Bohemia.

27. Portrait of Charles I. P. 1432.

Set against the background of Whitehall, this portrait was published in Antwerp shortly after the King's execution in January 1649.

29–31 (opposite). Three costume studies. Left: Lord Mayor's wife. P. 1892. Centre: Countrywoman. P. 1891. Right: Merchant's wife. P. 1893.

Costume was the index of both rank and nationality at this time. Indeed laws were still occasionally passed to enforce the social significance of fashion and to ensure that the more ambitious members of the middle ranks of society did not wear materials considered superior to their station.

Popular curiosity about foreign and remote countries that grew steadily from Elizabeth's reign onwards often focused on the dress of the inhabitants as the revealing feature of national character: consider, for example, the costumed figures in the margins of many late sixteenth- and seventeenth-century maps who stand almost as personifications of their country. Hollar produced scores of these engaging little studies which were constantly in demand and certainly very cheap, as this note in Robert Hooke's dairy for 1678 shows: 'Bought Hollars 12 woemen, 6d.' These plates date from the 1640s.

28. Arundel: view of the town and castle. P. 955.

32. Covent Garden. P. 909 (reduced $27\frac{1}{2}$%).

Inigo Jones attempted to introduce the formal and spacious Italianate piazza into London with his design for Covent Garden, which he executed for the Earl of Bedford during the 1630s. The scheme was a speculative building venture by the Earl to provide 'houses and buildings fitt for the habitacons of *Gentlemen* and men of ability'. To provide the new quarter with a respectable focus Bedford agreed to establish a church, but an inexpensive one. The result was St. Paul's, which was one of the very few churches erected in London between the Reformation and the Restoration. Its severe Tuscan manner commanded much admiration as an example of the classical elegance that Jones first brought to English architecture. St. Paul's was burned down in 1795, but was rebuilt in conformity with the original design. Over the years the ground level of Covent Garden has been raised, obscuring the plinth on which Jones's church stood, so that it no longer dominates the square as intended.

33–36. Four of the twenty-six costume studies from *Ornatus Muliebris Anglicanus*, or *The Severall Habits of English Women* (1640).

37. A gentleman of the 1630s. P. 1997 (reduced $22\frac{1}{2}\%$).

38. Portrait of Inigo Jones. P. 1428.

Inigo Jones, the leading architect of Stuart England, was also a protégé of the Earl of Arundel, and he accompanied the Earl to Italy in 1614. As a result of this visit Inigo was able to examine the buildings of Roman antiquity and the modern work of Palladio at first hand, and thus acquire the experience that was decisive to his career as the first exponent of revived classical architecture in England. After his return he moved, like Hollar later, into the service of the King, though in a much more significant role, as Surveyor of Works, which gave him control of royal building plans and also the production of the extravagant masques which were the spectacular culmination of the Stuart theatre. With their close Royalist connections, Hollar and Jones must have been acquainted, and although the story of their being captured together at the siege of Basing House in 1645 is probably erroneous, it indicates their association would be no surprise.

The etching here is after the drawing by Van Dyck which is now in the Chatsworth Collection. (Van Dyck himself was also under Arundel's patronage at the start of his career in England.) Hollar's version was used as the frontispiece to Jones's only book, *Most Notable Antiquity of Great Britain, or Stone-Heng Restor'd,* published posthumously in 1655, in which Jones argues his belief that Stonehenge was a Roman temple, built in the Tuscan style and dedicated to the god Coelus.

P. 1790–3 (reduced $27\frac{1}{2}\%$).

39. The trial of Thomas, Earl of Strafford in Westminster Hall, 1641. P. 551 (reduced 20%).

In this companion piece to no. 41 (the two were probably issued together as a broadside), Hollar catches the intense claustrophobic atmosphere of one of the great trials of the seventeenth century, when the Parliamentary party first asserted its strength over the King's men by the successful impeachment of Strafford.

Dominating the crowd is Hollar's patron, the Earl of Arundel (figure E), seated immediately below the throne, which is significantly empty. Strafford is in the dock with his back turned, accompanied by the Lieutenant of the Tower. Hollar shows remarkable versatility in displaying so many different poses and expressions in the assembled mass of Lords and Commons.

40. Detail from the execution of Thomas, Earl of Strafford. P. 552 (enlarged 75%).

41. The execution of Thomas, Earl of Strafford, 1641. P. 552 (reduced 12½%).

Strafford along with Archbishop Laud was the principal agent of Charles I's attempt at personal rule during the 1630s, and both men had made themselves widely unpopular by their implementation of royal tyranny. Amongst the first acts of the Long Parliament which assembled in November 1640 was the arrest and impeachment of Strafford and Laud. Strafford was tried for treason in April 1641 and condemned; Charles capitulated before the hostility of his Parliament, giving his consent to the judgment on May 10th. Two days later Strafford was executed on Tower Hill before a rejoicing multitude. One may observe that the hastily erected stands were not entirely sufficient for their purpose: one section can be seen collapsing. From his place of confinement in the Tower Laud had watched his colleague go out to the fate that he himself would suffer in January 1645.

The German inscription on the plate gives some idea of the international interest taken in England's affairs at this critical time.

42. The large study of muffs and other finery. P. 1951.

43. Costume study from *Ornatus Muliebris Anglicanus*. P. 1778.

44–7. *The Four Seasons*. P. 606–9.

This set of four plates, published 1643–4, shows English costume appropriate to the different seasons.

44 (opposite). Spring. P. 606.

The courtly figure holds a bunch of tulips, whose cult was at its height at this period. Notice the cavalcade with runners on the right by the wall of the house, which has been tentatively identified as Tart Hall, built for the Countess of Arundel by Nicholas Stone in 1638, at the corner of Buckingham Gate.

45 (overleaf 1). Summer. P. 607.

This is set in St. James's Park, where one may observe the gentry taking their ease. In the background are the Banqueting House with part of Whitehall, and St. Paul's. The verses attached to another of Hollar's summer scenes explain the accessories:

'In Summer when wee walke to take the aire
Wee thus are veyld to keep our faces faire,
And lest our beautie should be soyl'd with sweate,
Wee with our ayrie fannes depell the heate.'

46 (overleaf 2). Autumn. P. 608.

A matronly figure with feathered fan. The setting is Albury Park.

Welcom sweet Lady you doe bring
Rich presents of a hopefull Spring
Spring
That makes the Earth to looke so greene
As when shee first began to teeme.

How Phœbus, crowns our Sumer dayes
With stronger heate and brighterrayes

Summer

Her louely neck, and brest are bare,
Whilst her fann doth coole the Ayre.

As Autumes fruit doth mourne and wast
And if not pluckt it dropps at last

Autumne

So of herselfe (she feares) she shall,
If not timely gatherd, fall.

The cold, not cruelty makes her weare
In Winter, furrs and Wild beastshaire

Winter

For a smoother skinn at night
Embraceth her with more delight.

47 (left). Winter. P. 609. From *The Four Seasons*.

The absorbing background scene shows Cornhill with the tower of the Royal Exchange. The small tower-like building on the extreme right was known as the Tun; built in 1283, it was used as a jail for rowdy citizens. The plumes of smoke remind us that even in the seventeenth century smoke had become such a nuisance in London that Evelyn wrote a discourse, *Fumifugium* (1661), with a plan for refining the city's air.

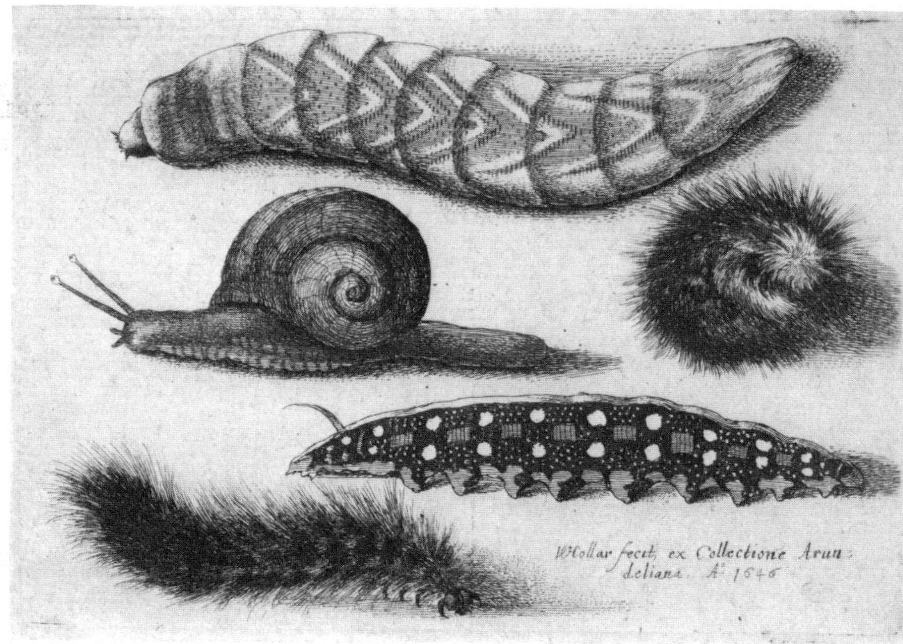

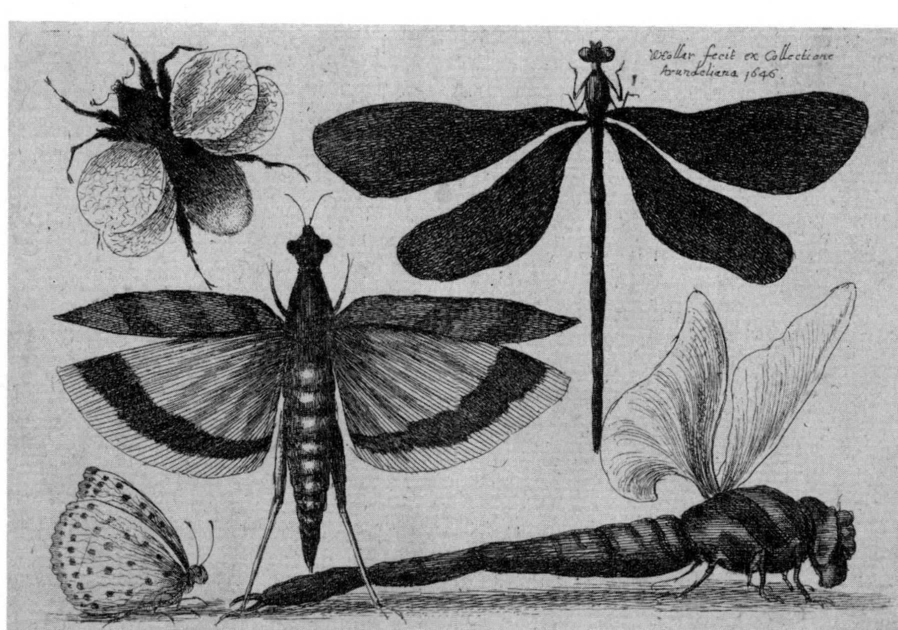

48–50 (right). Three studies from Hollar's *Muscarum Scarabeorum* . . . series (title and eleven etchings: P. 2164–75).

This set of insect studies, drawn from specimens in Arundel's 'Cabinet of Curiosities', was published in Antwerp in 1646. The variety of textures represents a considerable challenge to the etcher; the prints are among the triumphs of Hollar's art.

51. The Royal Exchange. P. 1036.

The Royal Exchange, built by Sir Thomas Gresham 1566–7 on the model of the Antwerp Burse, was the centre of British commercial activity. The merchants who crowded its Italianate courtyard represented trading interests from all over Europe and beyond. 'At every turn, a man is put in mind of Babel, there is such a confusion of languages,' wrote Dekker in 1607. Hollar's eye for national costume enables us to catch something of the internationalism of the scene: two Muscovite merchants in their furred caps stand in the left foreground, turbaned Turks are in the centre of the crowd, and representatives from Antwerp and Amsterdam, Venice and Vienna, are distinguishable. A woman selling broadsheets wanders through the crowd in the foreground. The composition of this print may well have been influenced by Aegidius Sadeler's engraving of The Vladislav Hall of Prague Castle (1607), which shows a similar multi-nationed scene of commerce.

On the first floor, above the cloisters, was The Pawn – rows of stalls selling all manner of fine and rare commodities. In the niches over the arcading stood the statues of the English monarchs from the time of Edward the Confessor. The one most clearly visible on the right, that of Charles I, was torn down after his execution in 1649, and its pedestal inscribed with the words 'Exit tyrannus regum ultimus' – 'The tyrant is gone, the last of the kings.' On the corners of the building, and on the tower, stood gigantic grasshoppers, the crest of the Greshams. The Exchange was destroyed in the Great Fire.

The scene here is High 'Change; another etching by Hollar (P. 907) shows the Exchange out of hours, the resort of strolling couples and playing children.

Through the south door on the left one catches a glimpse of Cornhill.

There are three states of the Exchange print: 1. This version. 2. With a medallion of Gresham's head depending from the cartouche. 3. With the English arms in place of the dedication, and dated 1668.

Honoratissimo Domino,
PRÆTORI REGIO sive MA
iori, Iohanni Wollaston Equiti,
Amplissimoq & Prudentissimo Sena
tui, Nobilissimæ & Florentissimæ Rei
publicæ Londinensis, &c. Hanc
tabulam a Wenceslao Hol
lar Bohemo, delineatam
& Aqua forti æri insculpta
ipse Author humillime
dedicat A° 1644
...YRSA LONDINENSIS,
vulgo
...all Exchange of London
...otum celebrata per orbem,
...c minor Vrbis Honos
...oc opus ELISABETHA
...cier esse suum
...nerces hic Gallus Iberus
...g convenIunt
...pit area murus
...endet Imaginibus
...chris habitata puellis
... transposuisse PAPHON
H Pecham
Lo heere the Modell of Magnificence,
Th EXCHANGE of LONDON thorough EVROPE fam'd,
Erected first by GRESHAMS greate expence,
And by the Roial'st Queene the ROYAL namd
The mother Antwerps farre exelling, where
But emptines is seene or trifles sold
Arabian odors, Silkes from SERES heere,
Pearles Sables, fine linnen Iewels, clothes of gold
And what not rare or rich our kinges take places
Without, Within a World of beauteous faces,
...hed & such Pillors as the rest
All which could not bee heere conveniently exprest
W: Hollar fecit Londini, Anno 1644.

52–9. The long view of London from Bankside.
P. 1014 (reduced 30%).

Hollar must have been preparing the material for this remarkable view over a considerable time before he left England in 1644, and it seems probable that he concentrated on this project in the two years following his patron's departure to Antwerp in 1642 as the best means of acquiring a wide reputation and securing his future as an artist. Its publication in London would certainly have established him as incomparably the finest etcher or engraver in the country. Instead, he had to take his sketches to Antwerp, where he etched the plates. Published in Amsterdam in 1647, the view was dedicated to Princess Mary of Orange, the daughter of Charles I.

The realistic presentation of the metropolis goes oddly with the baroque accessories that were then fashionable. On the left is the figure of Justice, surrounded with images of commerce, agriculture and arms. Rather ironically, considering the date, beneath her sword lies the image of the Crown supported by the Law.

Amongst the landmarks that are named on the view, moving from left to right:

Scotland Yard was a part of Whitehall which took its name from the fact that the Kings of Scotland or their ambassadors used sometimes to lodge there.

Suffolk House stood by Charing Cross, and was later known as Northumberland House when it passed from one family to the other. It was rebuilt towards the end of the sixteenth century, and survived until the end of the nineteenth.

York House, when Hollar drew it in the 1640s, belonged to the 2nd Duke of Buckingham, whose father, the notorious favourite of James and Charles, had built it in about 1625 after he had succeeded in acquiring Old York House from Sir Francis Bacon. As the name indicates, the old palace had been the London property of the Archbishops of York, who in turn had received it from Queen Mary in compensation for Whitehall, their original residence that had been confiscated by Henry VIII. The northern prelates chose not to occupy it, but let it to the Lord Keepers of the Great Seal as their official residence. Hence Sir Nicholas Bacon lived here, and died here in 1579. His son Francis was born here in 1561. Buckingham pulled down the medieval structure for something more in keeping with his position as the most influential man in the land, but only the section we see here was completed. The furnishings rivalled those of Arundel House further along the Strand, for Buckingham acquired an instant and superlative art collection by purchasing Rubens's private treasury of paintings and antiques, which included 19 Titians, 13 Veroneses, 17 Tintorettos, 3 Raphaels, 3 Leonardos and 13 canvases by Rubens himself. This assemblage was dispersed as quickly as Buckingham had obtained it, by order of Parliament in August 1645, and York House was given to General Fairfax. It was dismantled in the 1670s.

Durham House. The London residence of the Bishops of Durham, it passed through a number of hands after the Reformation. Sir Walter Raleigh lived here, and afterwards the house was acquired by the Earls of Pembroke.

53. The long view of London (cont.).

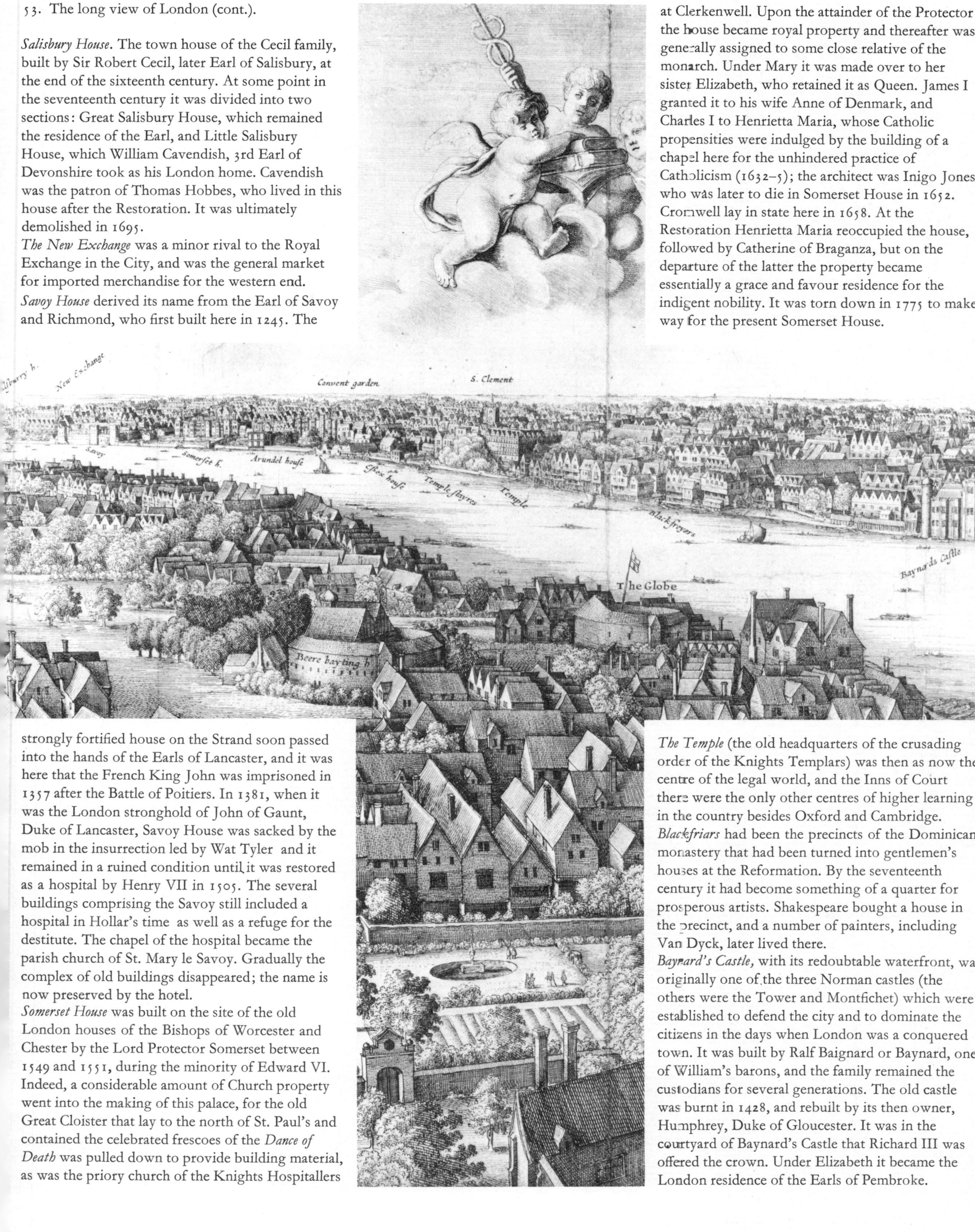

Salisbury House. The town house of the Cecil family, built by Sir Robert Cecil, later Earl of Salisbury, at the end of the sixteenth century. At some point in the seventeenth century it was divided into two sections: Great Salisbury House, which remained the residence of the Earl, and Little Salisbury House, which William Cavendish, 3rd Earl of Devonshire took as his London home. Cavendish was the patron of Thomas Hobbes, who lived in this house after the Restoration. It was ultimately demolished in 1695.

The New Exchange was a minor rival to the Royal Exchange in the City, and was the general market for imported merchandise for the western end.

Savoy House derived its name from the Earl of Savoy and Richmond, who first built here in 1245. The strongly fortified house on the Strand soon passed into the hands of the Earls of Lancaster, and it was here that the French King John was imprisoned in 1357 after the Battle of Poitiers. In 1381, when it was the London stronghold of John of Gaunt, Duke of Lancaster, Savoy House was sacked by the mob in the insurrection led by Wat Tyler and it remained in a ruined condition until it was restored as a hospital by Henry VII in 1505. The several buildings comprising the Savoy still included a hospital in Hollar's time as well as a refuge for the destitute. The chapel of the hospital became the parish church of St. Mary le Savoy. Gradually the complex of old buildings disappeared; the name is now preserved by the hotel.

Somerset House was built on the site of the old London houses of the Bishops of Worcester and Chester by the Lord Protector Somerset between 1549 and 1551, during the minority of Edward VI. Indeed, a considerable amount of Church property went into the making of this palace, for the old Great Cloister that lay to the north of St. Paul's and contained the celebrated frescoes of the *Dance of Death* was pulled down to provide building material, as was the priory church of the Knights Hospitallers at Clerkenwell. Upon the attainder of the Protector the house became royal property and thereafter was generally assigned to some close relative of the monarch. Under Mary it was made over to her sister Elizabeth, who retained it as Queen. James I granted it to his wife Anne of Denmark, and Charles I to Henrietta Maria, whose Catholic propensities were indulged by the building of a chapel here for the unhindered practice of Catholicism (1632–5); the architect was Inigo Jones, who was later to die in Somerset House in 1652. Cromwell lay in state here in 1658. At the Restoration Henrietta Maria reoccupied the house, followed by Catherine of Braganza, but on the departure of the latter the property became essentially a grace and favour residence for the indigent nobility. It was torn down in 1775 to make way for the present Somerset House.

The Temple (the old headquarters of the crusading order of the Knights Templars) was then as now the centre of the legal world, and the Inns of Court there were the only other centres of higher learning in the country besides Oxford and Cambridge.

Blackfriars had been the precincts of the Dominican monastery that had been turned into gentlemen's houses at the Reformation. By the seventeenth century it had become something of a quarter for prosperous artists. Shakespeare bought a house in the precinct, and a number of painters, including Van Dyck, later lived there.

Baynard's Castle, with its redoubtable waterfront, was originally one of the three Norman castles (the others were the Tower and Montfichet) which were established to defend the city and to dominate the citizens in the days when London was a conquered town. It was built by Ralf Baignard or Baynard, one of William's barons, and the family remained the custodians for several generations. The old castle was burnt in 1428, and rebuilt by its then owner, Humphrey, Duke of Gloucester. It was in the courtyard of Baynard's Castle that Richard III was offered the crown. Under Elizabeth it became the London residence of the Earls of Pembroke.

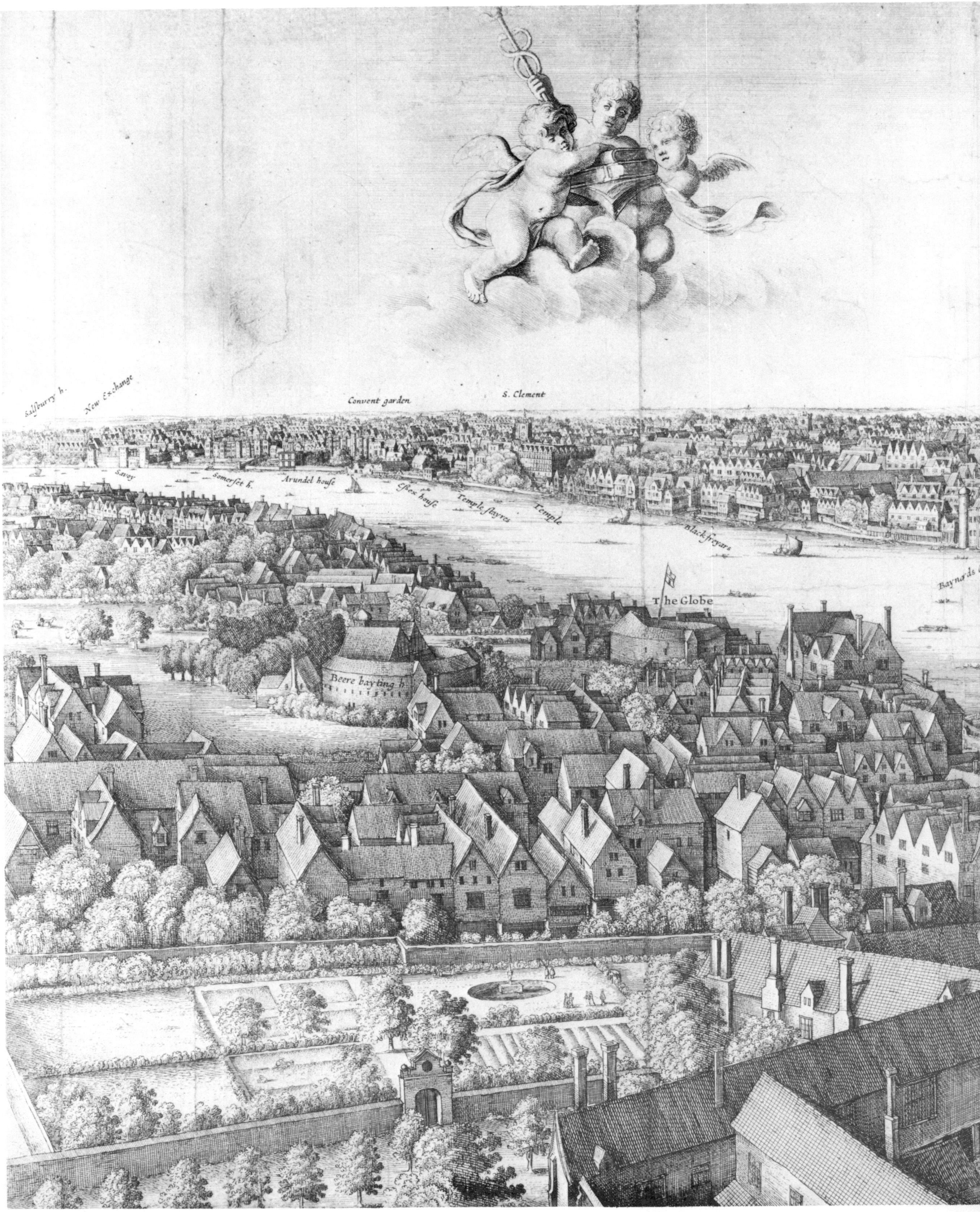

54. Uninterrupted view of plate 53.

55. The long view of London (cont.).

The view is taken from the top of St. Mary's, Southwark. In the foreground is the impressive medieval complex of Winchester House, the residence of the Bishop of Winchester until 1628, thereafter transformed into apartments. The fine gardens of the palace were built over in 1663, but the house remained until it was destroyed by fire in 1814.

The Three Cranes were regarded as marvels of Elizabethan technology; they were installed to lift the tuns of of wine on the Vintry wharf. Only two appear to remain at the time of this view.

56. The long view of London (cont.).

The Stiliard had been the headquarters of the German and Hanseatic merchants in London. The name was probably derived from the steel yard or metal beam that was used for weighing imported goods here. The Hall of the Merchants of Hanse contained two large and important paintings by Holbein: *The Triumph of Riches*, and *The Triumph of Poverty*. The merchants were expelled from England in 1598–9, and thereafter the Stiliard became a provision centre for the navy.

Coleharbour was a large block of tenements.

The Old Swan was where people of a cautious disposition used to alight when travelling downstream in order to avoid the perils of shooting the bridge. They would walk round and rejoin their boat on the other side.

57 (opposite). The long view of London (cont.).

Old London Bridge, overcharged with its mass of houses, on which smaller parasitic houses seem to cling and hang out in every direction and at every level, was one of the civic curiosities of Europe. The spectacular Tudor building in the centre, with its arcades and galleries and decorations of beams, was known as Nonsuch House, from its affinities with Henry VIII's palatial extravagance of that name in Surrey.

The numerous broad piers of the bridge effectively half-dammed the Thames at this point, and caused a dangerous rush of water under the arches which was one of the hazards of navigation on the river. An ingenious entrepreneur in Elizabeth's reign had exploited the unusual force of flow under the bridge by installing a large water-wheel in the first arch which was used to pump water from the river into the city.

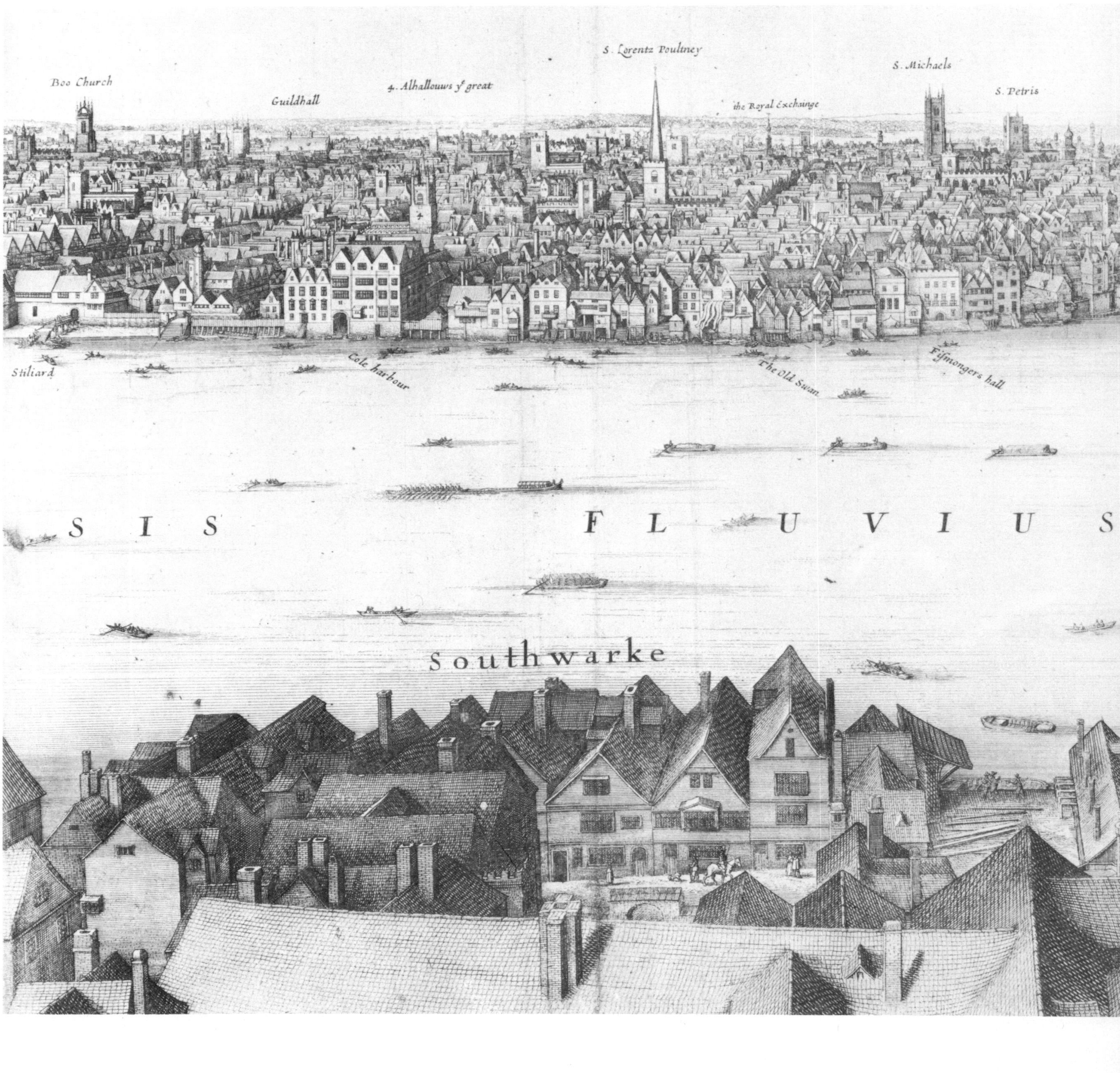

nes
2. Gray Church
S. Dunston in the East
J. Alhallows barking
Lyon kay
Billings gate
Costomhouse
THE BRIDGE.

58. The long view of London (cont.).

Beyond the bridge the port began, and some idea of the enormous mercantile prosperity of London can be gained from the mass of shipping that stretches far out to the horizon. Notice the ship being careened in the middle of the river east of the Tower.

The city soon merged into the fields; there is a windmill close to the Tower, and several more are visible behind the spire of St. Laurence Poultney.

In the sky float a series of inferior allegorical figures suggestive of the worldwide trade of the City of London. The group of putti with the lion-skin on the left may represent Africa; the next group represents learning and trade. The swift-footed Mercury was the patron of merchants, who, like him, circled the globe on their rapid errands; he is balanced by the figure of Fame with her trumpet. The lamentable group with parrot and jewels is perhaps an image of the Indian trade, while the little Indian leading an ostrich stands, rather confusedly, for America. On the right reclines the river god of the Thames, with all the wealth of Billingsgate pouring from his urn.

59. The long view of London (cont.).

60. The theatres on Bankside (detail of nos. 53/4).

In this small section of Bankside which lay outside the puritanical jurisdiction of the City of London the theatres flourished until their suppression by Parliament in 1642.

Although at first sight it seems that this is the clearest picture of the Globe to survive, one should beware, for a study of documents concerning the sites and features of the theatres indicates that Hollar has confused the labels of the Globe and the 'Beere bayting h[ouse]'. The confusion probably derives from Visscher's map of 1616 which Hollar used as a model for the general panorama and evidently also for the naming of some of the buildings; Hollar's own drawings for the view were not marked with names, and when he came to etch the plates in exile he apparently followed Visscher's labels, which were wrong. The bear-baiting ring had in fact been demolished in 1613–14, and was replaced in 1614 by the Hope Theatre which was designed to be used both for plays and for bear-baiting, so Visscher's label was already out of date in 1616, as well as misapplied. Thus the circular building with the flag entitled 'The Globe' in Hollar's etching in fact represents the Hope Theatre, and the larger building called the 'Beere bayting' is the Globe. The double-gabled roof which projects half way across the enclosure would form the ceiling or 'heavens' of the stage and provide a loft for celestial activity; the size of the projection indicates that it must have been supported on pillars. Shakespeare's theatre, the first Globe, had burned down in 1613; this, then, is the second Globe, built in 1614 and pulled down in 1644, which establishes the latest date by which Hollar could have made his drawings for the Long View.

(For a full account of the confusion of theatres, see I. A. Shapiro, 'The Bankside Theatres: Early Engravings', *Shakespeare Survey* 1, 1948.)

61. Deal Castle, from *Divers Views after the Life* (n.d.). P. 936.

62. The cliffs of Dover, from *Divers Views after the Life* (n.d.). P. 926.

Nos. 61 and 62 (right, above) are taken from a series of miniature views of South Coast castles which appeared in a little collection called *Divers Views after the Life*, by W. Hollar, published by P. Tempest. There is no date on the album; the dates on individual etchings range from 1642 to 1676.

63. Jersey, Elizabeth Castle, 1651. P. 924.

64. Hollow Tree. P. 979.

An old note on the British Museum copy states that this is a tree in Langley Park near Windsor, but the copy in the Royal Library at Windsor is part of a broadsheet proclaiming it to be the Hollow Tree at Hampstead, which is most probably the correct location. The trunk had a spiral staircase cut into it, and twenty people could be accommodated in the gallery at the top. The tree continued to flourish.

Since this etching is dated 1653 and seems to have been executed as an advertisement for a local phenomenon, it reinforces the evidence that Hollar had returned from Antwerp to London by this time.

The dates of 1651 on no. 63 (left) and 1650 on another view of the same subject (P. 923) suggest that Hollar joined the British court in exile, which was on the island at that time. Both Charles II and the Duke of York were there, and Hollar seems to have left Antwerp and followed his former royal pupils.

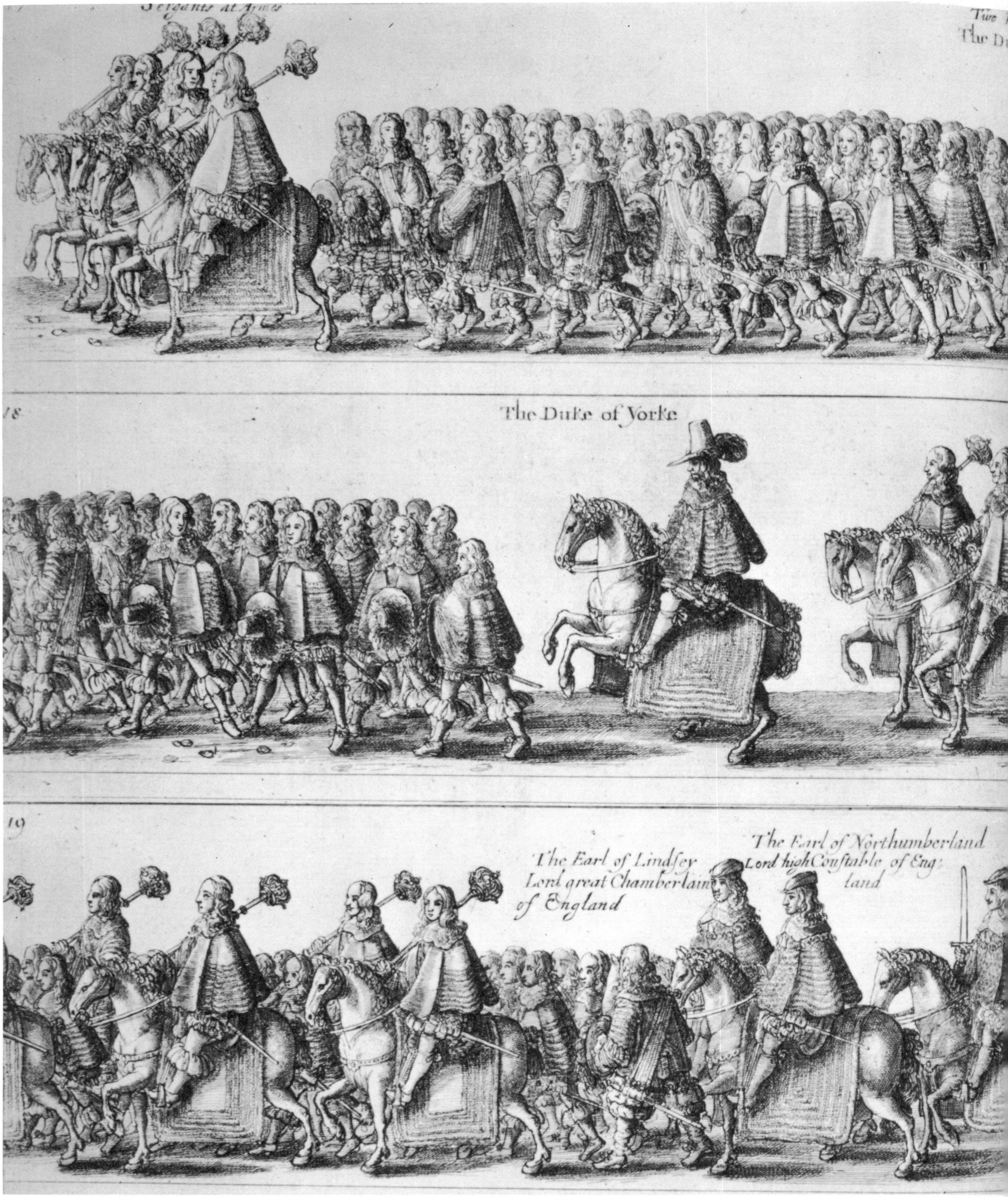

65. [from] The Coronation procession of Charles II, from Ogilby's *The Entertainment of His Most Excellent Majestie Charles II* (1661). P. 571 (reduced 10%).

The Restoration meant the return of magnificence to London after the subdued fashions of the Commonwealth. The traditional hierarchies march in splendour to Westminster Abbey in April 1661 as if the Interregnum had never occurred. This plate forms part of the processional sequence in John Ogilby's commemorative book. Hollar's ability to animate and vary the figures in a crowded scene adds an engaging touch of drama to Ogilby's narrative.

The Duke of Aquitaine
The Gentleman Usher
with the Black Rod
Garter principal
King of Arms
The Lord Mayor
of London
17
Sergants at Armes
18
Suffolk,
Footmen
Pages
Gentlemen Pension

66. The Coronation of Charles II in Westminster Abbey, from Ogilby's *The Entertainment of His Most Excellent Majestie Charles II* (1661). P. 575 (reduced 35%).

John Evelyn also recorded the memorable day: 'Anthems and rare musique playing with Lutes, Viols, Trumpets, Organ, Voices. . . Then, with the Crowne Imperial on his head, accompanied with all the nobility in the former order, he went upon blew cloth, which was spread and reached from the West dore of the Abby, to Westminster Stayres, where he tooke Water in a Triumphal barge to White-Hall, where there was extraordinary feasting.' (*Diary*, 23 April 1661.)

67. Portrait of Sir William Dugdale. P. 1392 (reduced 5%).

After Hollar returned from Antwerp in 1652, Dugdale (1605–86) became his most reliable and enduring patron. He was an untiring antiquarian whose ample volumes were founded in the detailed study and interpretation of rolls, charters, registers and genealogies which here wall in his world of learning. Besides those works that Hollar illustrated extensively – *History of St. Paul's* (1658), to which this portrait is the frontispiece, *Monasticon Anglicanum* (I, 1655; II, 1661; III, 1673), and *The Antiquities of Warwickshire* (1656), which provided a pattern for subsequent county histories – Dugdale's major antiquarian publications were his study of the English legal system, *Origines Juridicales* (1666) (with three plates by Hollar), and *The Baronetage of England* (1675–6).

68 (right). Title page for *Monasticon Anglicanum* (1655). P. 2660.

This is the title page of the work, written by William Dugdale and Roger Dodsworth, for which Hollar supplied so many architectural illustrations. The design in the manner of a baroque façade (which was not considered incompatible with a medieval subject) contains scenes exemplifying the growth and decay of monasticism. The emotional bias of these vignettes is decidedly in favour of medieval piety; the devout monarch on the left contrasts markedly with Henry VIII, whose tyrannical gesture of dissolution leaves no doubt as to the book's attitude towards him. The upper vignettes record the antiquity and pristine piety of the Church, and its defence of its rights against King John. Gregory and Augustine appear as the saints responsible for the spread of Christianity to England, for Gregory as Pope decided on the conversion of England and Augustine was the missionary who undertook the work.

Printed and sould by Iohn Overton at ye White horse in Little Brittaine

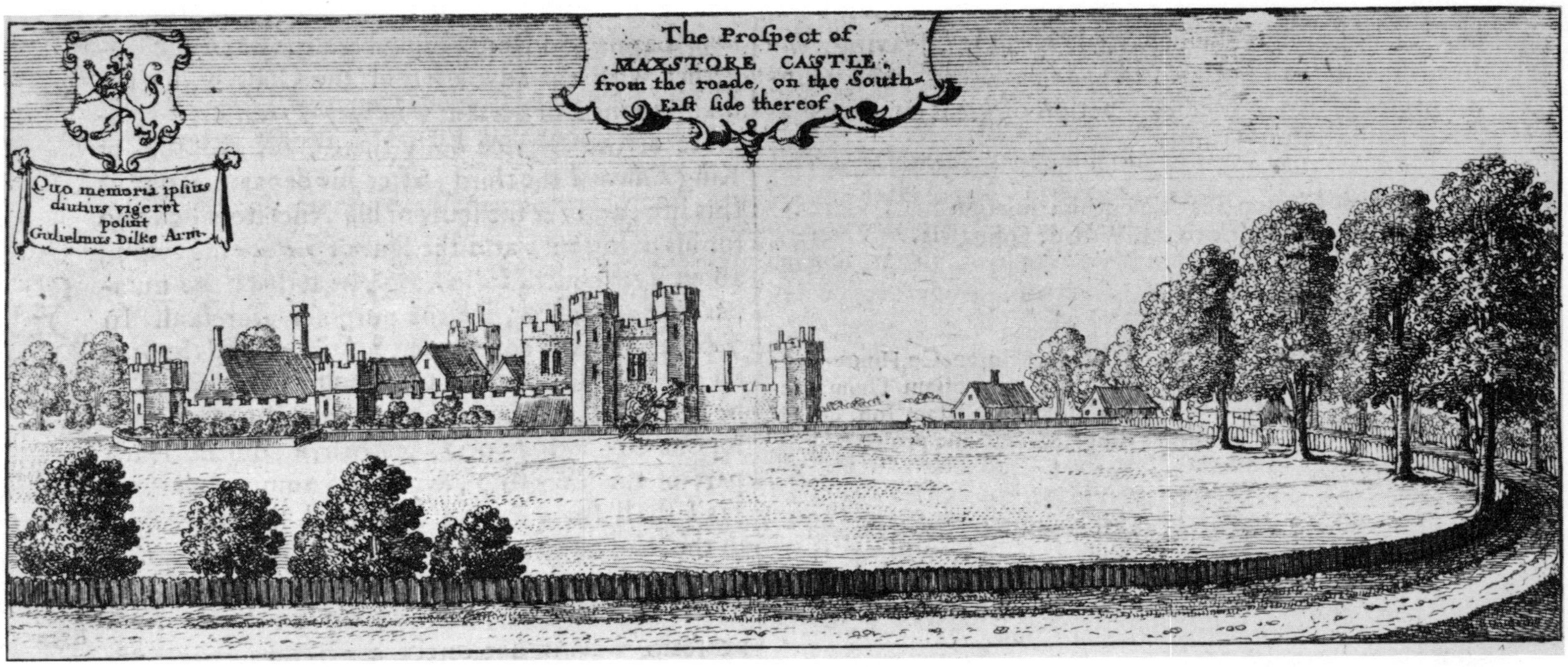

69. Maxstoke Castle, from Dugdale's *Antiquities of Warwickshire* (1656). P. 1045 (enlarged 10%).

This fortified manor was built in the fourteenth century and remodelled in the fifteenth by the Earl of Stafford.

70. The Hospital or Priory of St. John of Jerusalem, from Dugdale's *Monasticon*, vol. II (1661). P. 1031 (reduced 40%).

This priory in Clerkenwell was the seat of the Knights Hospitallers of St. John, an order that originated in the Crusades. Built in 1100, it was sacked by Wat Tyler's mob in 1381, rebuilt, and finally suppressed in 1541. In the seventeenth century the hospital seems to have been used for private residences; the view of the courtyard shows that modern doorways had been recently added when Hollar drew the scene.

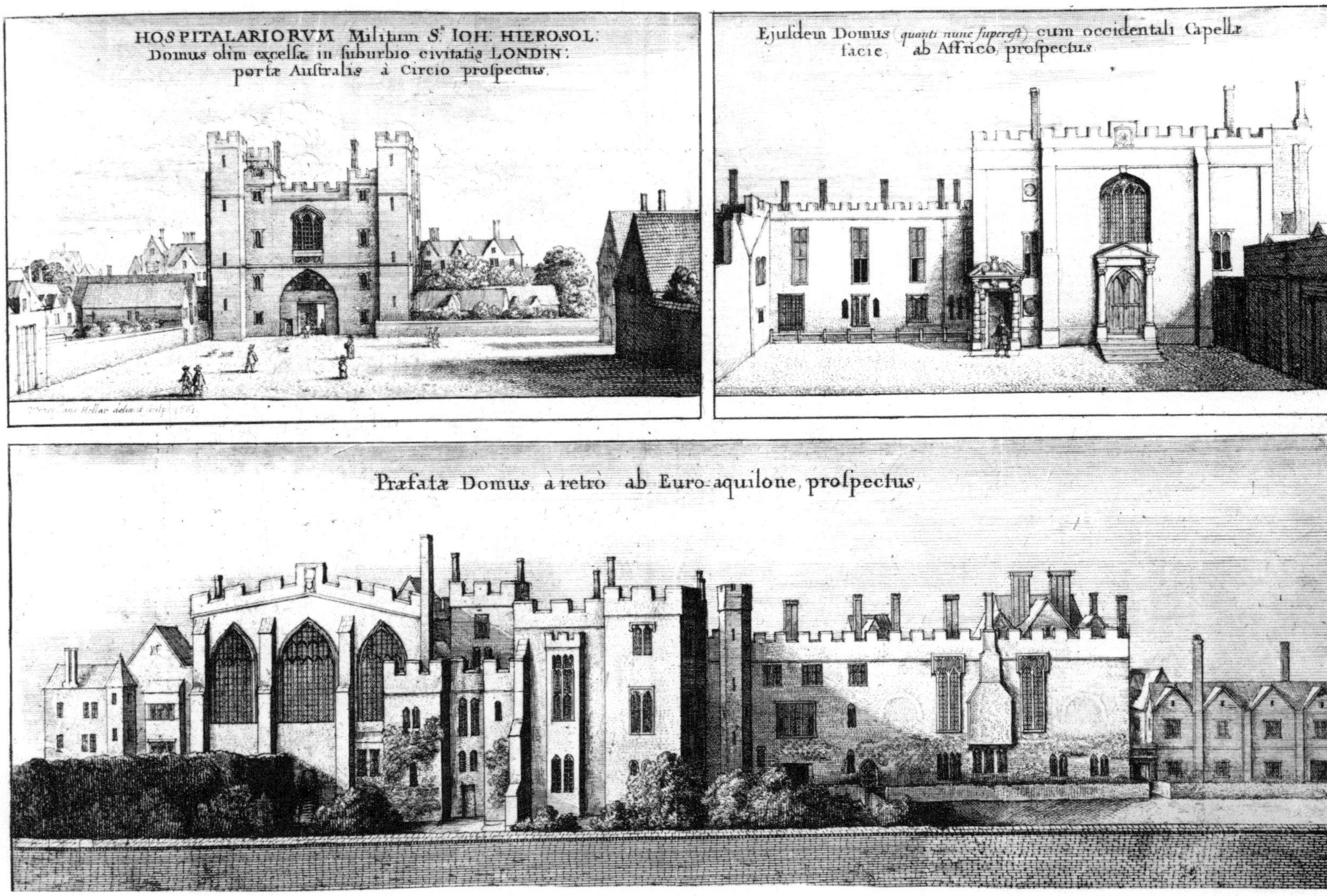

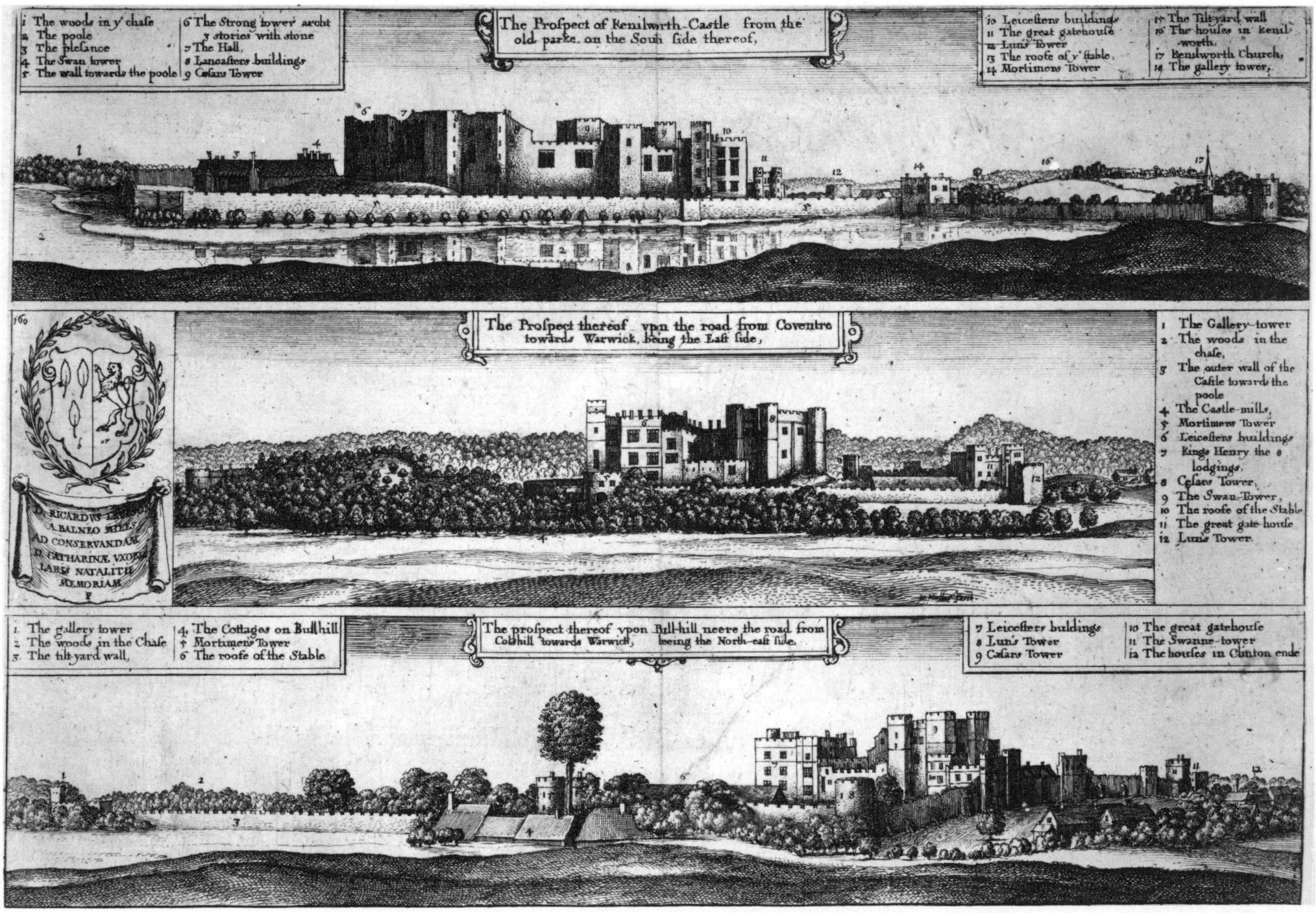

71. Kenilworth Castle, from Dugdale's *Antiquities of Warwickshire* (1656). P. 986 (reduced 25%).

The old royal castle of Kenilworth, transformed from a fortress into a palace by John of Gaunt, entered its period of greatest splendour when Elizabeth gave it to her favourite, the Earl of Leicester, in 1563. The Queen was entertained here by Leicester in 1575 in one of the most prodigal of the Elizabethan feats of banqueting and pageantry. Kenilworth was occupied by the Parliamentarians during the Civil War; and in 1649, shortly before Hollar drew the castle, they blew up the keep and ruined the walls.

72. Langar House and Church, from Thoroton's *Antiquities of Nottinghamshire* (1677). P. 988 (reduced 25%).

73. Large bird's-eye view of West London. P. 1002 (reduced 20%).

A remarkably imaginative aerial view, showing superb command of perspective and scale. When one considers that this is not a panorama that could be drawn from a fixed point, like the long bird's-eye view of London (P. 1014), but purely an imaginative projection, then one may marvel at Hollar's control of his complicated subject.

This etching is extremely informative about the layout of the great mansions along the river: one sees what rambling collections of houses they were, and one notes too the variety of formal gardens they possessed – gardens that offered so much satisfaction and symbolism to their cultivators, both through the new rarities that could be grown there, and for the philosophical suggestiveness that gardens held in an age when the visible could easily be regarded as a map of the spiritual.

Hollar's view preserves a number of curiosities, such as the maypole in the Strand, on the site of the present church of St. Mary le Strand (maypole dancing was suppressed by the Puritans as being wanton and a pagan rite); and the waterhouse, the pyramidal structure at Strand Bridge, which raised water from the Thames to supply the city. A squad of soldiers can be seen exercising in Lincoln's Inn Fields, much used as a parade ground during the troubled years 1641–60. Close by them one can even make out clothes drying in the Fields. Cows can be seen grazing in the fields beyond Holborn. One recalls that Hollar was trained as a miniaturist, and the skills he learnt then form an essential part of his art of etching.

The copy of this plate in the British Museum is the only one known to survive. Hind suggests a date of c.1658, on the evidence of the state of building around Lincoln's Inn Fields.

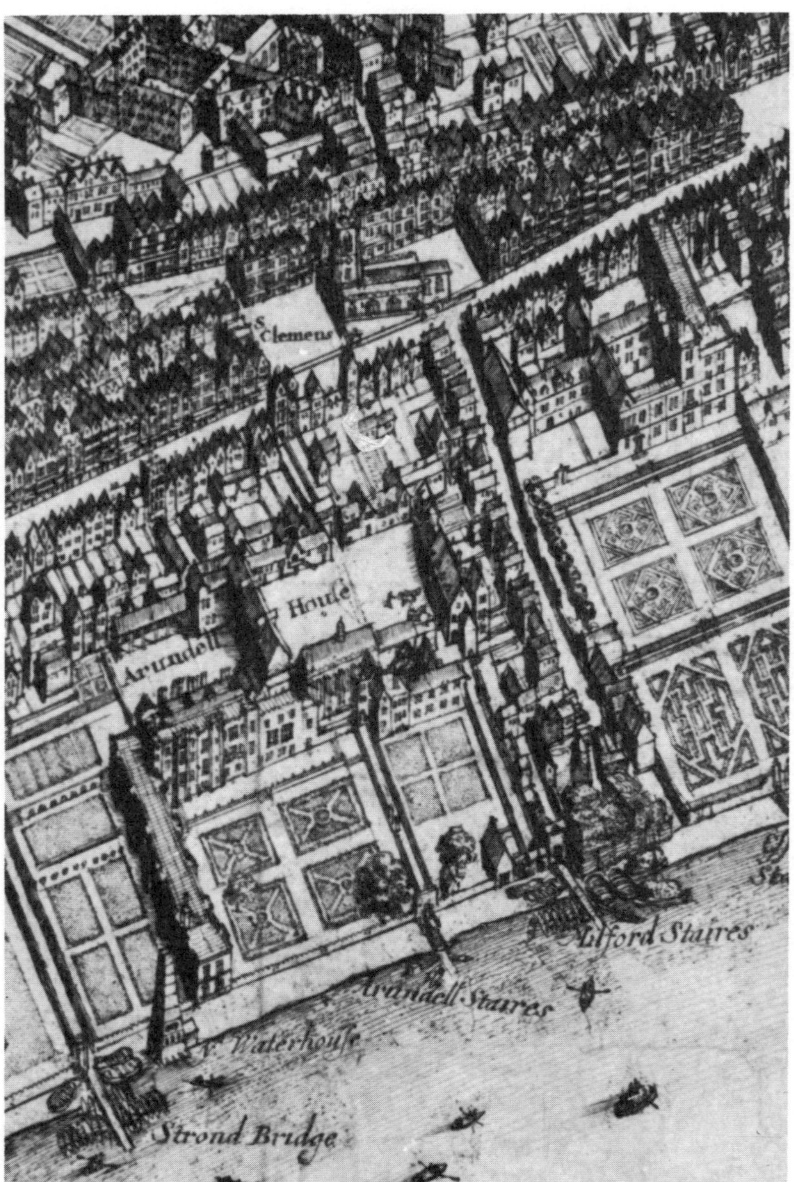

73A. Detail of P. 1002 (enlarged 150%).

Lincoln Inn
Fields
Lincoln
Inn
lesser
Lincoln Inn Fields
Piazza
in Coventgar
den
Somerset
house
Somerset House
Strond Bridge
Somerset Staires
Somerset Wharfe
Stronde
Bedford
house
The
Savoy
Arundel
House
Essex
Staires
Milford Staires
Arundell Staires

74. Frontispiece to James Howell's *Londinopolis* (1657). P. 1012.

As St. Mary Overy's appears in the picture, it must have been drawn from a more easterly point than the Long View. The Swan Theatre that stands out on Bankside was erected in 1595, and it was of this theatre that the visiting Dutchman De Witt made his famous sketch in 1596 that provides the main visual account of the interior of an Elizabethan playhouse. The Swan proved to be an unsuccessful theatre, and by 1632 it was described as 'now fallen to decay'; this being so, it seems odd that it should still be a prominent building twenty-five years later, at the time of the publication of *Londinopolis*. The most likely explanation is that Hollar made the sketch for this view or even etched the plate some time in the early 1640s.

75. The tomb of John of Gaunt, from Dugdale's *History of St. Paul's* (1658). P. 2292 (reduced 15%).

Son of Edward III and father of Henry IV, John of Gaunt was the only royal figure to be buried in St. Paul's Cathedral after the Conquest. He died in 1399, and was buried with his wife Blanche in this elaborate Perpendicular tomb by the High Altar.

154
ECCLESIÆ CATHEDRALIS.
S. PAVLI
AB OCCIDENTE PROSPECTVS.
CAROLVS D.G. MAGNÆ BRITANNIÆ FRANCIÆ ET HIB. REX TEMPLV DIVI PAVLI VETVSTATE CONSVPTV RESTITVIT

76. St. Paul's Cathedral, west front; from Dugdale's *History of St. Paul's* (1658). P. 1020.

The fabric of St. Paul's had deteriorated so much by the time of James I that a Royal Commission was established to consider the question of restoration. Members included the Duke of Buckingham, Francis Bacon and Inigo Jones, who was then Surveyor of His Majesty's Works. Estimates and plans were made, but there was little action until William Laud was appointed Bishop of London in 1628 and applied his energies to the scheme. A national subscription for the restoration was opened, and by 1632 enough money had been collected to permit the beginning of the work under the direction of Inigo Jones. As the principal exponent of the Renaissance manner in England, it was perhaps not surprising that he should wish to disguise the essential Gothic character of St. Paul's in an Italianate cloak, thus giving London a modern cathedral without the expense of total rebuilding. The Norman west front was completely remodelled in a heavily rusticated classical manner; the old portals were replaced by stately Roman doors, and the lancet windows were transformed into fashionable round-headed ones. To break up the Gothic roof-line, Jones introduced obelisks to frame the main gable and covered the aisle ends with large baroque scrolls. The most striking and admired addition was the sumptuous Corinthian portico which seems to have been regarded by contemporaries as the chief architectural glory of St. Paul's. Certainly King Charles was so impressed by the design that he undertook to bear the cost of its construction. Sixty-six feet high and 120 feet long, it was undoubtedly a dignified preface to the renewed building. Above the parapet were pedestals for statues of the cathedral's benefactors, but only the first two Stuarts, decorous in Roman costume, were ever installed. During the Commonwealth, when the cathedral suffered a variety of abuses, and when only the far east end of the choir was protected from vandalism (it was walled off for use as a preaching hall), the portico was considerably damaged by the building of shops beneath it. New attempts at restoration after the devastations of the Cromwellian period had hardly begun before the Great Fire effectively solved the problem of what treatment to adopt.

The two small western towers served as ecclesiastical prisons. The northern one was connected to the adjoining Bishop's palace; the southern one, known as the Lollard's Tower, was much used in the sixteenth century for the imprisonment of heretics.

77. St. Paul's Cathedral in flames.
P. 1028.
This vignette appeared in *Lex Ignea*, a sermon expounding the significance of the Fire preached by William Sancroft, Dean of St. Paul's, in 1666, and then published.

78. St. Paul's Cathedral, south side; from Dugdale's *History of St. Paul's* (1658). P. 1018 (reduced 10%).

The small building adjoining the south-west end of the nave was the parish church of St. Gregory, which had sheltered against the cathedral since Norman times. It was rebuilt in the seventeenth century in keeping with Inigo Jones's restyling. One section of the cathedral that was not renewed was the chapter house, which can be seen most unhappily and incongruously hemmed in behind its cloister wall.

One of the splendours of Gothic St. Paul's has been its great wooden spire rising to a height of 447 feet which had perished in a fire of 1561, to be replaced by this dull little cap.

(It is a measure of the reasonably tolerant climate of opinion in the later years of the Protectorate that both this plate and P. 1019 showing the north side were subscribed by the nephew of William Laud to celebrate his executed uncle's exertions at restoration.)

79. St. Paul's Cathedral, the crypt; from Dugdale's *History of St. Paul's* (1658). P. 1030 (reduced 40%).

The building of the new choir in the thirteenth century had necessitated the demolition of the parish church of St. Faith which stood in the way of the extension. In compensation, the western part of the crypt under the choir was given to the parishioners as their new church. The other half of the crypt beyond the wooden screen was the Jesus Chapel until it was made part of St. Faith's in 1557. Here preachers gave their sermons when bad weather prevented them from using the open-air pulpit, Paul's Cross.

During the Great Fire the booksellers of St. Paul's Churchyard used St. Faith's as a repository for their stocks, believing the crypt to be fireproof. The falling roof of the cathedral, however, cracked open the floor, and all was consumed; some of the leaves of burned books were blown, according to a contemporary account, as far as Eton.

127
DOMVS CAPITVLARIS S. PAV
Meridie Prospectus.
VERO NIL VERIVS.
Ne memoria domus Capitularis
(in qua ordo et disciplina Dei servientiū
non sterquilinia et stercora equorū acer
vari solebant) fori vænality luto subpedi
taretur, ALBERICVS de VERE, XX.us ejus
dem stirpis et agnominis Comes OXONII
hanceejusdem Domus prospectum,
pia magis posteritati commendari
curavit.

80. St. Paul's Cathedral, the cloisters and chapter house; from Dugdale's *History of St. Paul's* (1658). P. 1023 (enlarged 10%).

The cloisters and the octagonal chapter house were erected during the 1330s, and were unusual for being two-storey buildings. The print shows clearly how Inigo Jones had recased the old Norman nave with a classical facing, replacing the buttresses with pilasters and framing the windows in an Italianate manner.

81. St. Paul's Cathedral, the rood screen; from Dugdale's *History of St. Paul's* (1658). P. 1024 (reduced 15%).

The decorated stone screen containing the statues of eight English kings was erected in the middle of the fourteenth century. Over the screen there was originally a beam that supported the Great Rood, the wood carving of the Crucifixion that was removed at the Reformation. The plate shows the Norman work of the transept walls, and also reveals that the choir aisles had been filled in to help carry the weight of the tower.

Partis exterioris Chori, ab Occidente prospectus.
Hoc Monumentum æternitati sacrum esse voluit,
HENR. COMPTON,
Illustriss: Comitis Northamptoniæ
filius natu minimus
Cal: Febru:
An: CIↃ. IↃC. LVI
ria Troja,
Vel sicut formæ species sub schismate mentis
Instar Narcissi tenuem dissoluor in umbram,
Dabit Deus his quoq finem
Virg: Æneid: Lib 2.

NAVIS ECCLESIÆ CATHEDRALIS S. PAV
PROSPECTVS INTERIOR.

82 (left). St. Paul's Cathedral, the nave; from Dugdale's *History of St. Paul's* (1658). P. 1025 (reduced 25%).

The Norman nave of twelve bays was under construction throughout the twelfth century, and was only finally vaulted at the beginning of the thirteenth. The design of the bays shows some resemblance to those of the nave of Peterborough Cathedral.

By the sixteenth century, this part of St. Paul's, commonly known as Paul's Walk, had become virtually secularised, a resort for the fashionable and the idle, a place of trade and employment, and a general thoroughfare for merchandise. Various proclamations issued during the sixteenth and seventeenth centuries to re-establish the religious character of the nave failed to have any effect, and it remained a mixture of market and social centre. During the Commonweath the whole area was given over to the stabling of the horses of the Parliamentary troops.

83. St. Paul's Cathedral, the choir; from Dugdale's *History of St. Paul's* (1658). P. 1026 (reduced 55%).

Work on the new choir began in 1256, and involved the remodelling of the old Norman choir as well as the addition of eight bays to the east; the use of Purbeck marble against white pillars must have made the choir of St. Paul's resemble that of Lincoln, which was built at the same time. The focus of the east end was the great rose window, forty feet across, unique in English cathedral architecture. The wooden screen separated the Lady Chapel from the rest of the church; under the Puritans this part was the only section of St. Paul's preserved for religious services, being used as a preaching hall. Perhaps for purposes of clarity, Hollar has omitted the splendid monumental tomb of Sir Christopher Hatton, Queen Elizabeth's Chancellor, which occupied the second bay west of the screen on the south side.

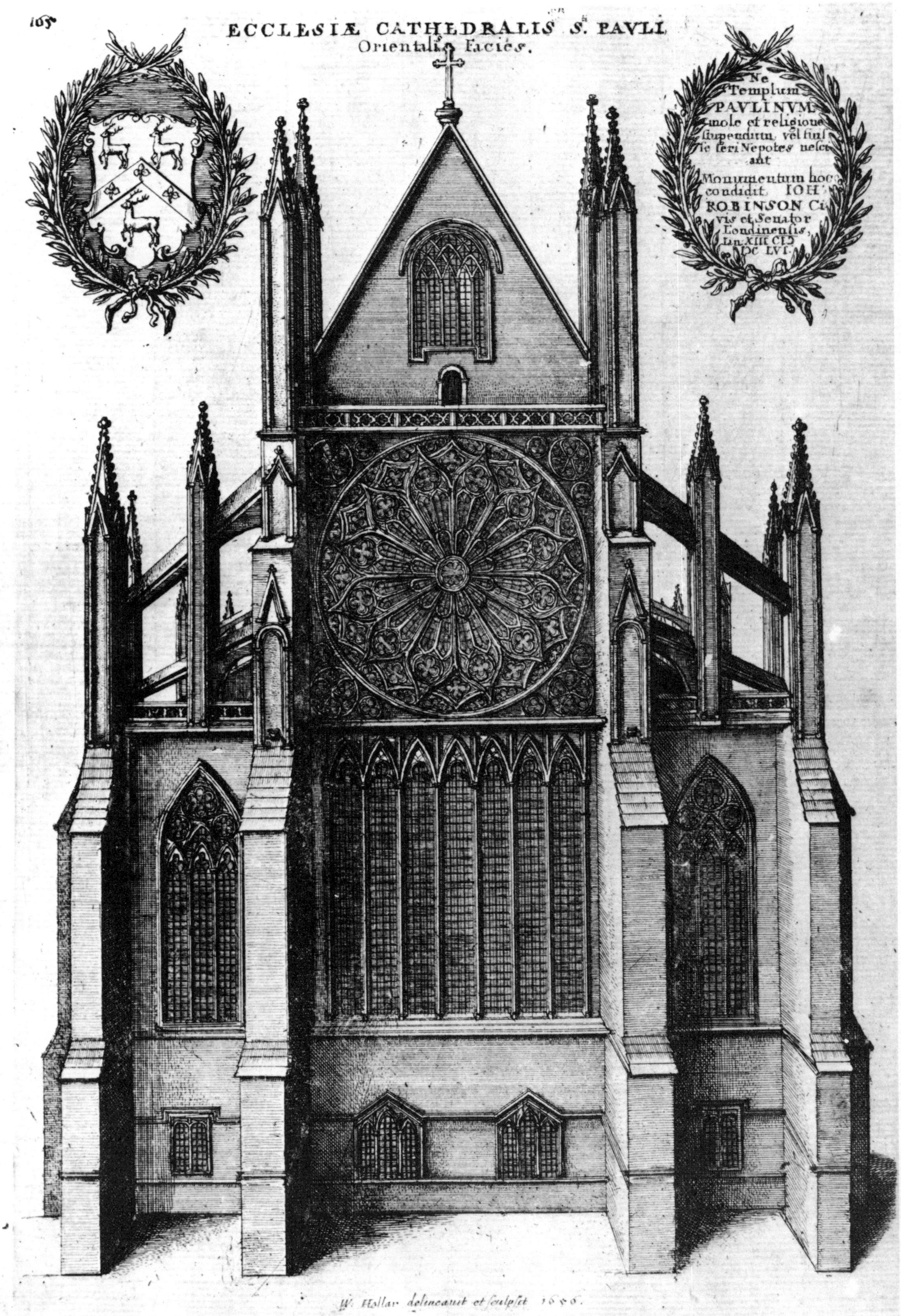
105
ECCLESIÆ CATHEDRALIS S.TI PAVLI
Orientalis Facies.
Ne
Templum
PAVLINVM
mole et religione
stupendum, vel fuis
se seri Nepotes nesci
ant
Monumentum hoc
condidit IOH:
ROBINSON Ci
vis et Senator
Londinensis,
Ian: XIII CIↃ
IↃC LVI.
W. Hollar delineauit et sculpsit 1656.

84. St. Paul's Cathedral, east end; from Dugdale's *History of St. Paul's* (1658). P. 1027.

This view shows the great rose window at the end of the choir, and also the remodelling of the transepts effected during the 1630s by Inigo Jones.

85. Funerary effigy of Dr. Donne, from Dugdale's *History of St. Paul's* (1658). P. 2277.

John Donne was a connoisseur of the phases of death, and approached his own with a lugubrious panache. When he observed himself entering his last decline,

'Dr. Donne sent for a carver to make for him in wood the figure of an urn, giving him directions for the compass and height of it; and to bring with it a board of the just height of his body. "These being got: then without delay a choice Painter was got to be in readiness to draw his Picture, which was taken as followeth. . . . Several Charcole fires being first made in his large Study, he brought with him into that place his winding-sheet in his hand, and, having put off all his cloaths, had this sheet put on him, and so tyed with knots at his head and feet, and his hands so placed, as dead bodies are usually fitted to be shrowded and put into their Coffin, or grave. Upon this Urn he thus stood with his eyes shut, and with so much of the sheet turned aside as might shew his lean, pale, and death-like face, which was purposely turned toward the East, from whence he expected the second coming of his and our Saviour Jesus." In this posture he was drawn at his just height; and when the picture was fully finished, he caused it to be set by his bed-side, where it continued, and became his hourly object till his death: and was then given to his dearest friend and Executor Doctor Henry King, then chief Residentiary of St. Paul's, who caused him to be thus carved in one entire piece of white marble, as it now stands in that Church.' Izaac Walton, *Life of Dr. John Donne* (1640).

This was the only monument from Old St. Paul's to survive the Fire unscathed. The sculptor was Nicholas Stone.

86–91. Views of rural Islington in 1665.

86. By the Waterhouse. P. 915.

87. By Islington, with distant view of St. Paul's. P. 916.

88. By Islington. P. 917.

89. On the north side of London. P. 918.

90. Waterhouse by Islington. P. 919.

91. The Waterhouse, with distant view of St. Paul's. P. 920.

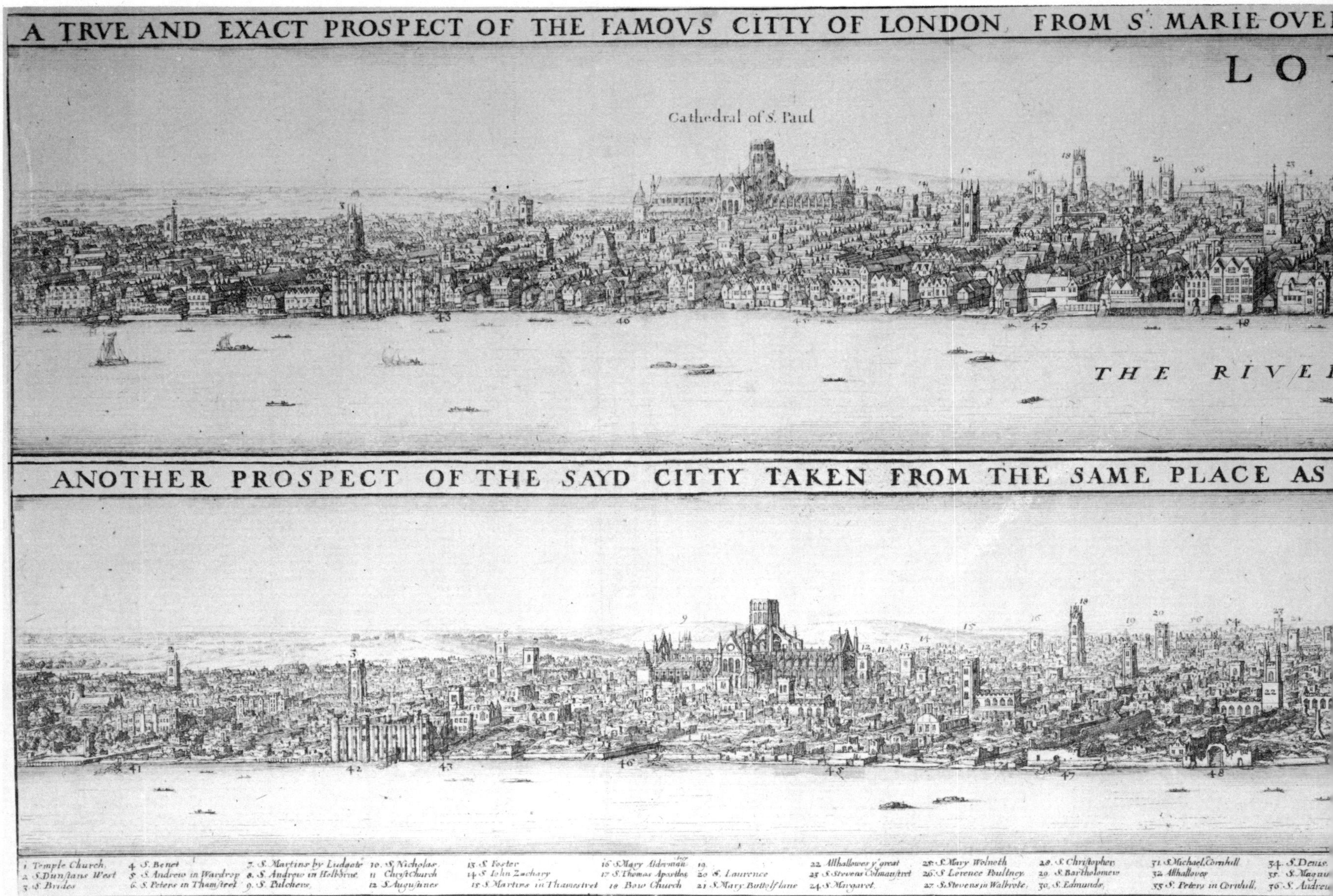

92. London before and after the Great Fire. P. 1015 (reduced 30%).

Hollar was particularly well placed to make this comparative record of the Fire, for he had on several occasions drawn the panorama of London from Southwark, and these drawings had become virtually overnight a record of the vanished city. He immediately exploited the situation by etching this new plate, a fascinating eyewitness memorial of the catastrophe. In five days, 2–6 September 1666, the Fire destroyed five-sixths of the City of London, from the Tower to Blackfriars, an area a mile and a half long and half a mile broad. It consumed 89 churches, 460 streets, and 13,200 dwelling houses, according to the inscription on the Monument. The crowded mass of wooden buildings in the upper view makes it easy to see why the flames spread so quickly.

What an extraordinary sense of desolation this lower scene transmits, with its dozens of gutted churches standing in a wilderness of ashes; even the river, now emptied of ships, looks forlorn. The huge shell of St. Paul's, which dominated the city in its ruin even more than in its prosperity, still remained substantial enough to tempt thoughts of rebuilding it, and not until 1673 was the decision finally taken to raze it. This etching also reminds us how close the countryside came to the Thames; the refugees did not have far to go to the safety of the fields.

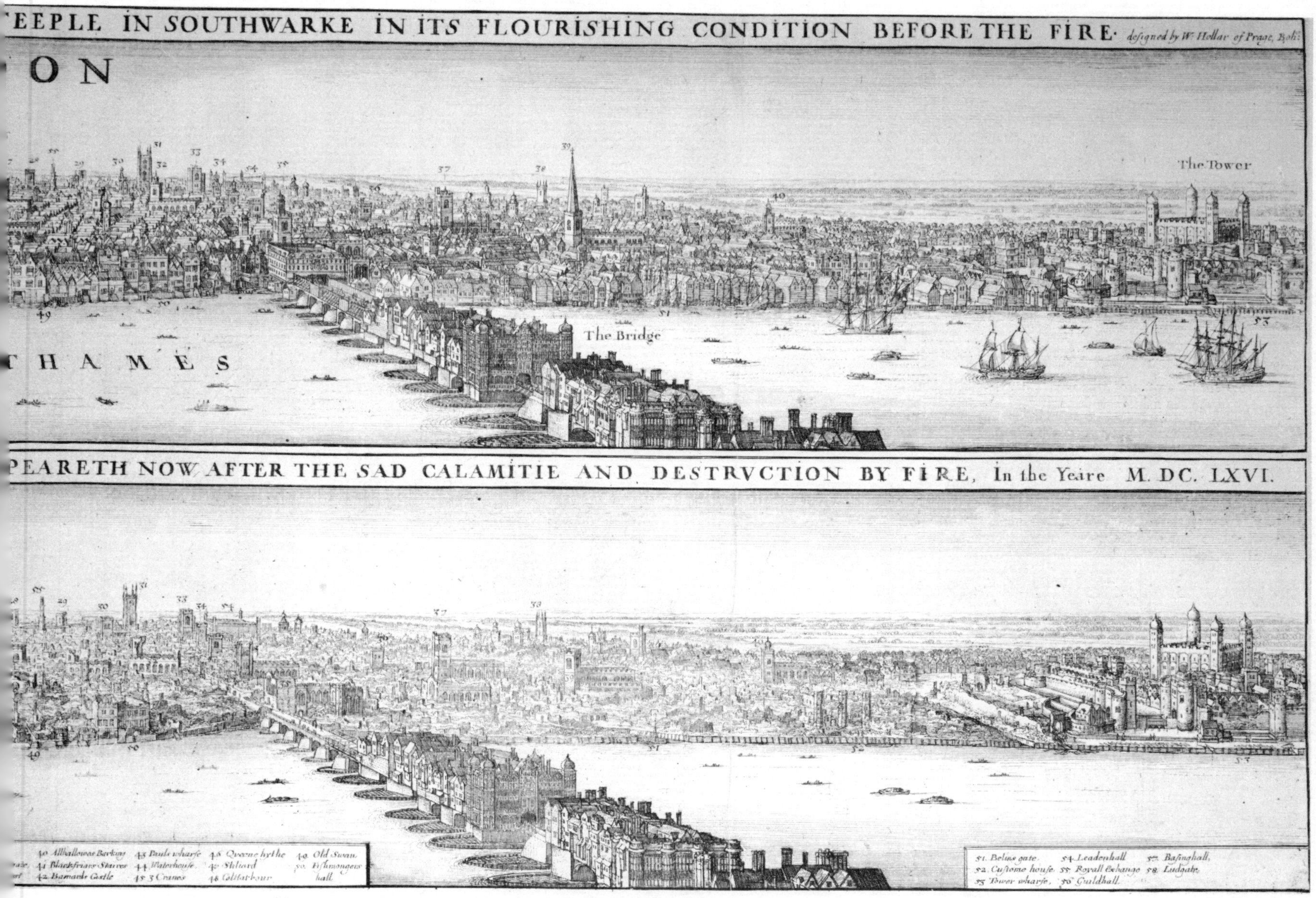

93 (below). Detail from survey of London burnt. P. 1006 (reduced 45%).

This impression of the Fire was included by Hollar at the top of the left-hand plate of his map of 1667, which – like the map shown overleaf (P. 1004) – was made presumably to help plan the reconstruction of London.

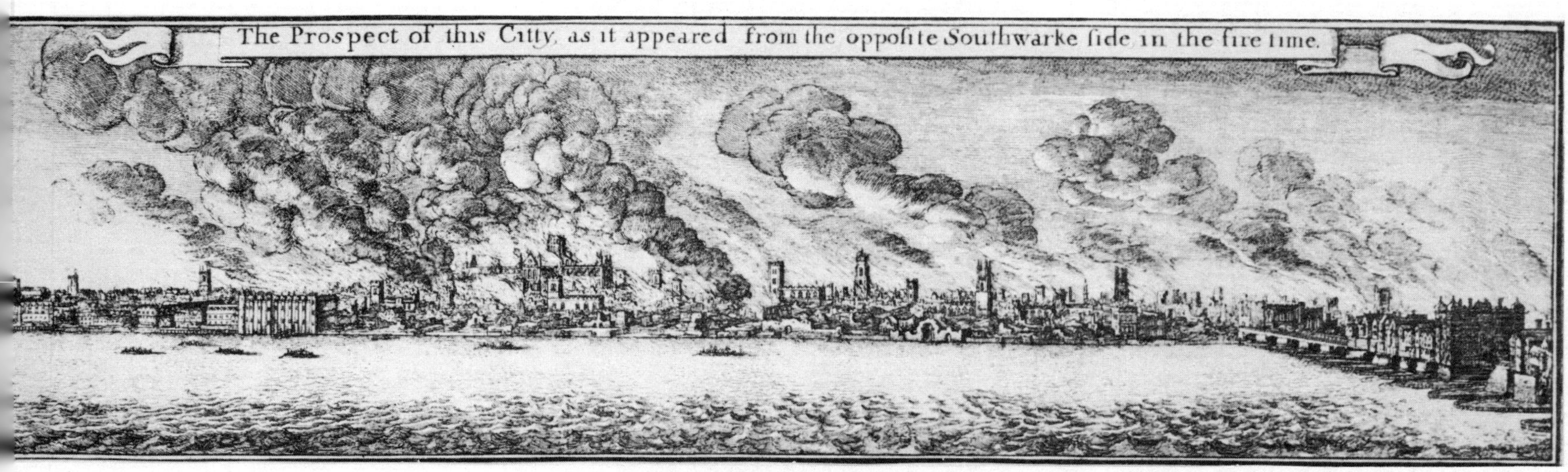

94. Map of London, dated 1666. P. 1004.

One of two maps that Hollar made showing the extent of London's destruction, presumably intended to aid those concerned with the planning of the new city. The speed with which the surveying and execution of the plate were carried out is characteristic of the urgency with which the reconstruction of the city was tackled: both Wren and Evelyn had submitted designs for rebuilding within a few months of the Fire.

A MAP or GROVNDPLOT of the Citty of London and the Suburbes thereof, that is to say, all which is within the Iurisdiction of the Lord Mayor or properlie call'd London by which is exactly demonstrated the present condition thereof since the last sad accident of fire. The blanke space signifeing the burnt part & where the houses are exprest, those places yet standig.
Sould by Iohn Overton at the White horse, in little Brittaine, next doore to little S. Bartholomew gate 1666.
Frisbury Fields
Artilery ground
Moore Fields
Spittle Fields
East Smithfield
Tower hill
Thames Street
The Tower
THA MES
Part of Southwarke
Annotations of the Churches, and other remarkable places in this Map.
1. Cathedrall of S. Paul,
2. Christ Church,
3 S. Michaell
4 S. Peters by Woodstreet
5 S. Foster,
6. S. Leonard,
7 S. Ann by Aldersgate
8 S. Michaell in Woodstreet,
9 S. Iohn Zachary
10 S. Olaves,
11 S. Mary Stayning,
12,
13 S. Mary Aldermanbery,
14 S. Michaell Bashaw,
15 S. Laurence,
16 S. Maudlins,
17 Allhallowas,
18 S. Martins in Irenmongers lane,
19 S. Olaves,
20 S. Mary Colechurch
21 S. Steven Colmanstreet
22 S. Mildred,
23 S. Margaret,
24 S. Christopher,
25 S. Bartholomew,
26 French Church,
27 S. Benet,
28 Augustine Fryars,
29 S. Martins Outwich,
30 S. Michaell in Cornhill,
31 S. Peters,
32 Allhallowes
33 S. Edmunds,
34 S. Clemens,
35 S. Nicholas,
36 S. Mary Wolnoth,
37 S. Mary in Canwike Street,
38 S. Stevens in Walbrooke,
39 S. Bennet,
40 S. Pancras,
41 S. Antholins,
42 Bow Church,
43 S. Matthew,
44 S. Austins,
45 S. Gregory,
46 S. Martins by Ludgate,
47 S. Andrew,
48 S. Benet in Thamstreet,
49 S. Peters,
50 S. Mary
51 S. Nicholas,
52 S. Nicholas Olaves,
53 S. Mary Somerset,
54 S. Iohn Evangelist,
55 S. Mildred,
56 Allhallowes,
57 S. Mary
58 S. Thomas Apostle,
59 S. Iohn Baptist,
60 S. Michaell,
61 S. Iames,
62 S. Martins,
63 S. Mary Buttolfs lane,
64 S. Swithens,
65 S. Mary in Bushlane,
66 Allhallowes great,
67 Allhallowes the lesser,
68 S. Laurence Poultney,
69 S. Mich: by Crooked lane,
70 S. Magnus,
71 S. Margaret,
72 S. Leonard,
73 S. Bennet,
74 S. Dennis,
75 S. Margaret Patteus,
76 S. Andrew Hubart,
77 S. Georges,
78 S. Bottolphs,
79 S. Mary hill,
80 S. Dunstan East
81 Allhallowes Barking,
82 S. Olaves,
83 Allhallowes Fanch: St:
84 S. Catharin Colemans,
85 S. Cath: Creed Church,
86 S. Andrew Vndershaft,
87 S. Hellins
88 Ethelborough,
89 Allhallowes in the Wall,
90 S. Bottolphs Bishgate
91 S. Bottolphs Aldgate,
92 S. Brides
93 Temple Church,
94 S. Dunstans West,
95 S. Andrew in Holborne,
96 S. Pulchers,
97 S. Bartholomew great,
98 S. Bartholomew the lesse,
99 S. Bottolphs by Aldersgate,
100 S. Giles by Cripplegate,
A Ludgate
B Newgate
C Aldersgate,
D Cripple gate,
E Moore gate
F Bishopsgate
G Aldgate,
H Essexhouse,
I the Temple
K Dorset house,
L Bridewell,
M Baynards Castle,
N Christ Ch: Clorst:
O Hosp: S. Barth:
P Charterhouse,
Q Guildhall.
R the Stokes
S Royall Exchange,
T Gresham Colledge,
V Leadenhall,
W Dukes Palace,
X Custome house
Y Bedlame,
Z Sion Colledge,
a Temple Staires.
b Whi: friars Staires
c Black fryars Staires,
d Puddle dock.
e Paules wharfe,
f Broken wharfe,
g Queene Hythe
h 3 Cranes,
i Stiliard,
k Coldharbour,
l Old Swan,
m Belins gate,
n Tower wharfe,
o Artilery Yard,
10 20 30 40 Perches
This length is one English mile from one end to the other,

95. Lincoln Cathedral, east end; from Dugdale's *Monasticon*, vol. III (1673). P. 994.

The composition shows a fine sense of massing. The subscriber's plate indicates the heightened consciousness of time's ravages so characteristic of this age.

SIÆ LINCOLNIENSIS FACIES.
Vt nec per Temporis ru:
inas aliquando, aut Incendij;
nec, quod sævius depopulatur,
Sacrilegij (quod absit) prorsus
intereat Ecclesia Lincolniensis
Tabulam hanc
GUILIELMUS
EPISCOPUS LINCOLNIEN:
Sculpendam Curavit, et Æterni:
:tati Vovit. Æ. Dni. 1672.
sic

96. Lincoln Cathedral, from the north; from Dugdale's *Monasticon*, vol. III (1673). P. 996.

Hollar here seriously underestimates the massiveness of the western towers. The donor of this plate, Dean Honeywood, has requested Hollar to restore the spire of the central tower that was blown down in 1547 in order that the cathedral may be seen in its original perfection.

97. Detail from York Minster, west front; from Dugdale's *Monasticon*, vol. III (1673). P. 1087 (reduced 50%).

98. Salisbury Cathedral, west front; from Dugdale's *Monasticon*, vol. III (1673). P. 1060.

The detached bell tower on the left was destroyed by Wyatt in his scheme of reconstruction begun in 1798.

dralis
MENSIS
tilone
In piorum hujus Ecclesiæ fundatorum memoriam, hoc posuit,
HVGO SPEKE DE HASEL-BVRY, in agro WILTON:
Baronettus,

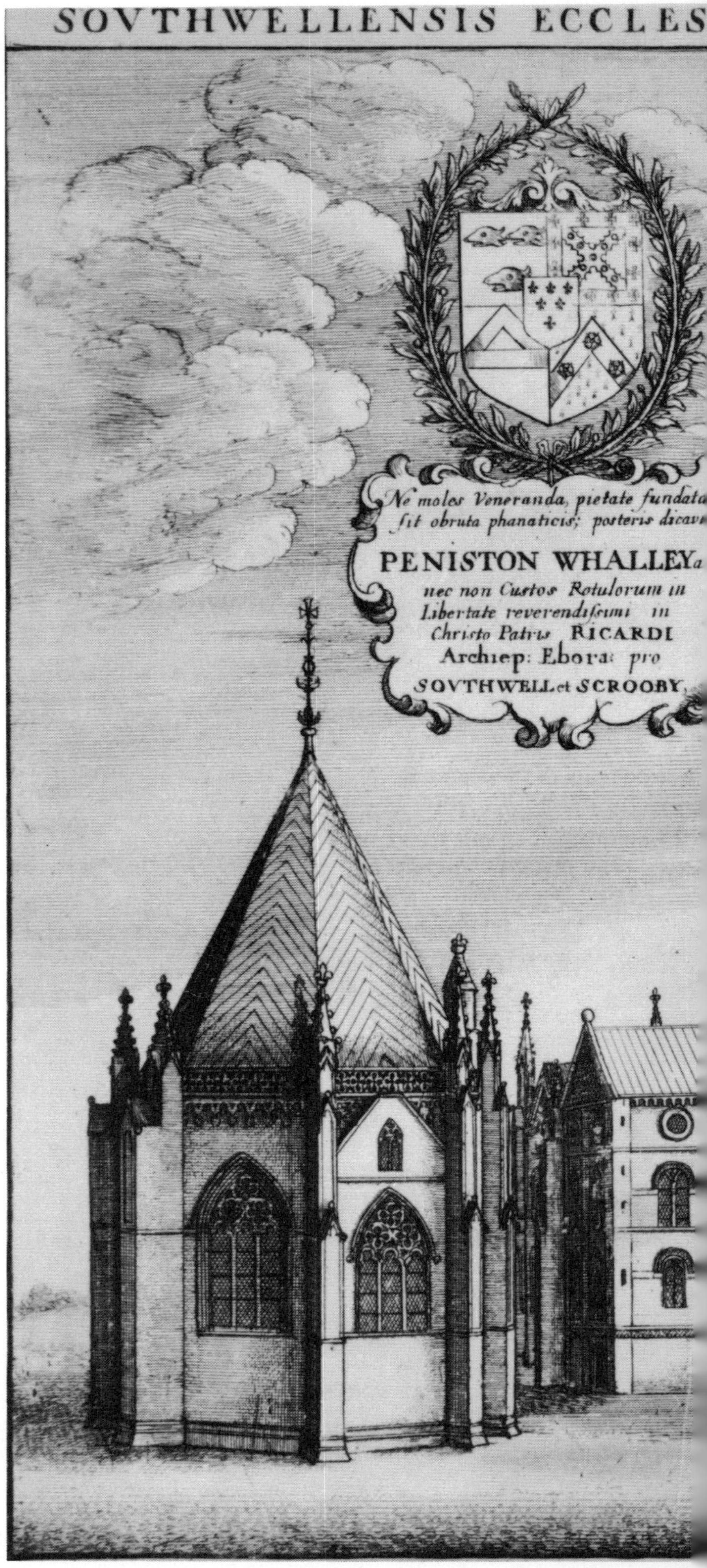

99. Southwell Minster, from the north-west; from Dugdale's *Monasticon*, vol. III (1673). P. 1063 (enlarged 15%).

This plate, etched after a design by Richard Hall, was re-used in Thoroton's *Antiquities of Nottinghamshire*. It shows the old steeply pitched gables on the towers.

COLLEGIATÆ A BOREA ZEPHIRO PROSPECTVS.
Ric: Hall delin: W: Hollar sculp

100. Lichfield Cathedral, west front; from Dugdale's *Monasticon*, vol. III (1673). P. 990 (reduced 5%).

101–4. London and Westminster from Lambeth. P. 1013 (reduced 40%).

This prospect shows how thoroughly rural the south side of the river was. Lambeth village rapidly fades out into the Marsh. Lambeth Palace occupies the foreground.

The manner of the design is very close to the long London view of 1647 (P. 1014), but the plate seems to have been touched up by an alien hand in the area rebuilt after the Fire.

102. London and Westminster from Lambeth (cont.). P. 1013 (reduced 40%).

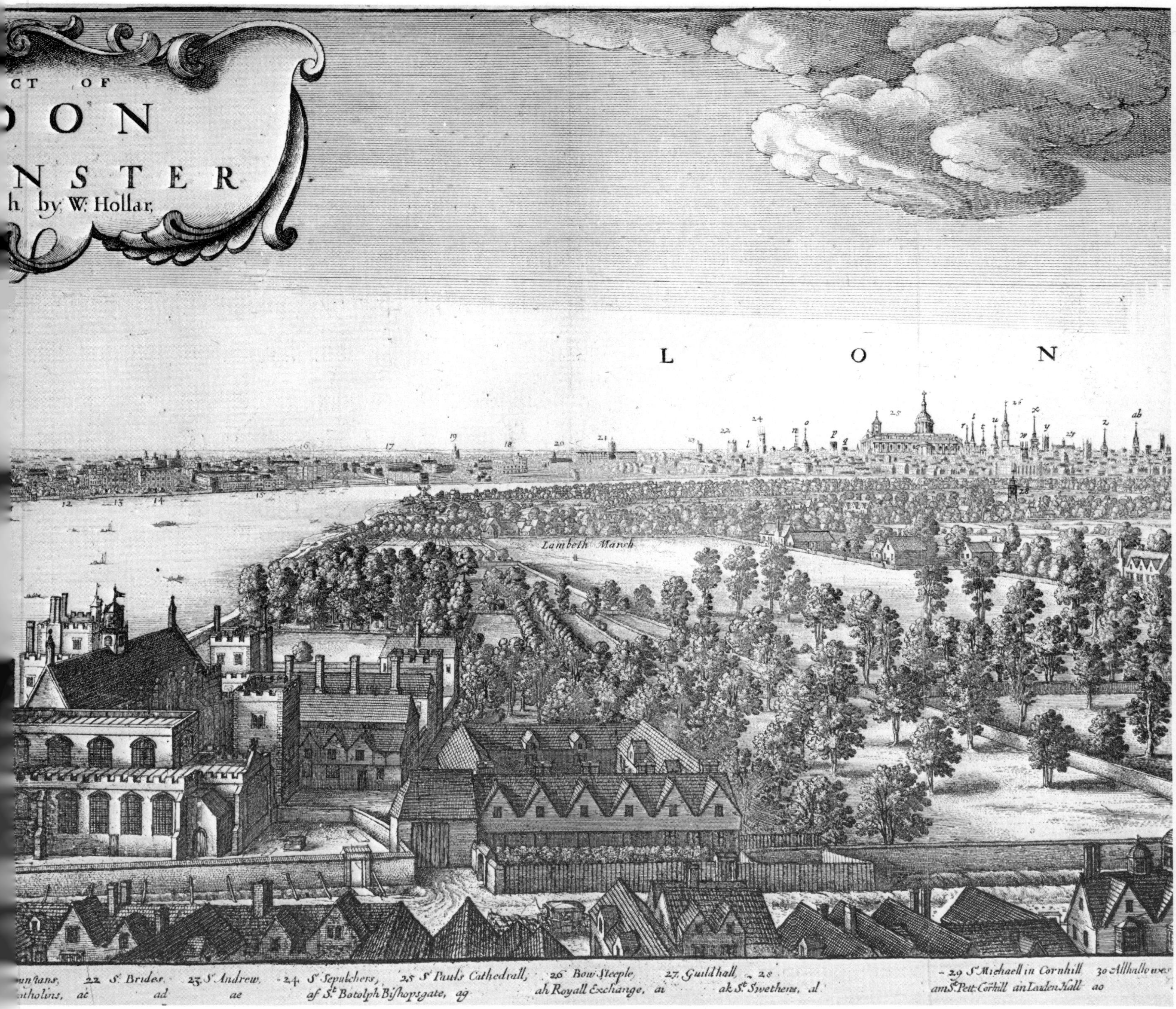

CT OF
DON
NSTER
h. by W. Hollar,
L O N
Lambeth Marsh
22 St. Brides,
23 St. Andrew,
24 St. Sepulchers,
25 St. Pauls Cathedrall,
26 Bow Steeple,
27 Guildhall,
28
29 St. Michaell in Cornhill
30 Allhallowes
af St. Botolph Bishopsgate,
ah Royall Exchange,
ak St. Swethens,
am St. Pett: Cornhill
an Leaden Hall

104. London and Westminster from Lambeth (cont.). P. 1013 (reduced 40%).

105. Title page for the *Polyglot Bible* ed. B. Walton (1656). P. 2649 (reduced 20%).

Baroque constructions like this lent themselves equally to altars, tabernacles, tombs or title pages. This title to the *Polyglot Bible* is a particularly fine specimen of literary architecture, which has here been turned to theatrical use with a stageful of Old Testament characters, with Moses and Aaron prominent under the elaborate Corinthian porticoes. Above, Peter and Paul guard a pentecostal scene in which the one Word descends into many tongues.

S.S.
BIBLIA
Polyglotta.
Complectentia Textus Originales
HEBRAICOS
CHALDAICOS
HEBRÆO-SAMAR.
GRÆCOS.
Versionumq. Antiquarum
SAMARIT. GRÆC. SEPT
CHALDAIC. SYRIACÆ
LAT. VULG. ARABICÆ
ÆTHIOPIC. PERSICÆ
Quicquid comparari poterat.
Ex
M.SS. Antiquiss. undiq. Conquisitis optimisque Exemplaribus impressis summa fide collatis.
Edidit
Brianus Waltonus. S.T.D.
Anno. M.DC.LVI.
I. Webb inv.
W. Hollar fecit.

The Road from
LONDON TO BARWICK
BRITANNIA
VOL. I
or an
Illustration
of ye Kingdom of
ENGLAND
and dominion of WALES
By a
Geographical & Historical
Description
of the Principal
ROADS.

106 (left). Frontispiece to John Ogilby's *Britannia* (1675). P. 2681 (reduced 15%).

This was a book on the roads of Britain. The design shows travellers setting out in various directions from one of London's gates – though very possibly an imaginary one, for only the coat of arms on the portcullis indicates that this is supposed to be the boundary of London. The foreground is filled with various cosmographers and students of travel. The one-wheeled object being pushed off the right of the scene may have been an instrument for measuring distance.

The designer of this frontispiece was Francis Barlow, Hollar the etcher.

107. Frontispiece to Thomas Sprat's *History of the Royal Society* (1667), after a design by John Evelyn. P. 459.

The Royal Society had not much history to record in 1667, having been in existence only seven years. Sprat's work was essentially an advertisement for the aims of the group of 'experimental philosophers' who met together to investigate the properties of the physical world and to further the understanding of all natural phenomena. Their members included Christopher Wren, who at this time was Professor of Astronomy at Oxford; Robert Boyle, the sceptical chemist; the astronomer and mathematician Seth Ward, who later became Bishop of Exeter; Robert Hooke, skilled in physics, chemistry, mechanics and microscopy; and men of varied, abstruse and humane learning such as Dryden, Aubrey, Pepys and Evelyn. In spite of the formidable intelligence of the Society, the whole conception of experimental science was regarded by a large part of educated men as a futile endeavour, worthless in comparison with the study of moral philosophy, and even as an impious probing of God's secrets. As late as 1726 Swift in *Gulliver's Travels* could still ridicule the activities of the Royal Society as 'nonsense on stilts'.

Evelyn's design shows Fame crowning a bust of the Society's patron Charles II, who is here looking thoroughly Augustan. The figure on the right is Bacon, who laid the foundations of experimental science, and whose work the Society intended to continue and expand; on the left is Lord Brouncker, the first President.

The pieces of scientific equipment that lie everywhere are almost all instruments of measurement for astronomical, chemical, barometric and ballistic experiments. Notice the gentleman in the field behind kneeling at an early telescope.

108. Inset from portrait of Thomas Hobbes (1588–1679), after J. Baptiste Caspar, 1665. P. 1417.

Hobbes was the most important English philosopher of his age. *Leviathan*, his radical study of the body politic and the social contract, was published in 1651. His materialist theories earned him the reputation of an atheist from a society not yet prepared to accept his secular assumptions.

Aubrey can add some colour to this portrait:

'In his old age he was very bald (which claymed a veneration) yet within dore, he used to study, and sitt bare-headed, and sayd he never tooke cold in his head, but that the greatest trouble was to keepe-off the flies from pitching on the baldness.

'Face not very great; ample forehead; whiskers of yellowish-redish, which naturally turned up – which is a signe of a brisque witt. Belowe he was shaved close, except a little tip under his lip. Not that nature could have afforded a venerable beard, but being naturally of a cheerfull and pleasant humour, he affected not at all austerity and gravity to look severe. He desired not the reputation of his wisdome to be taken from the cutt of his beard, but from his reason.

'He had a good eie, and that of a hazell colour, which was full of Life and Spirit, even to the last. When he was earnest in discourse, there shone (as it were) a bright live-coale within it.'

It is quite possible that the title page of Hobbes's *Leviathan* was designed by Hollar. The original unsigned pen and ink drawing in the British Museum is in a manner that is remarkably like Hollar's. Hobbes, who already knew Hollar, was living in Paris, and could easily have contacted him in Antwerp in 1650–1. The engraved title page of the first edition (1651) is certainly not by Hollar, and is much coarser than the original drawing, with several alterations.

109. Detail from the title page to John Johnson's *Academy of Love* (1641). P. 2673 (enlarged 30%).

The title page preserves the memory of a sociable scene in some great lord's hall. Cupid, the great lord himself, introduces a gallant to an elegantly dressed gentlewoman; the sequel may be divined from the title.

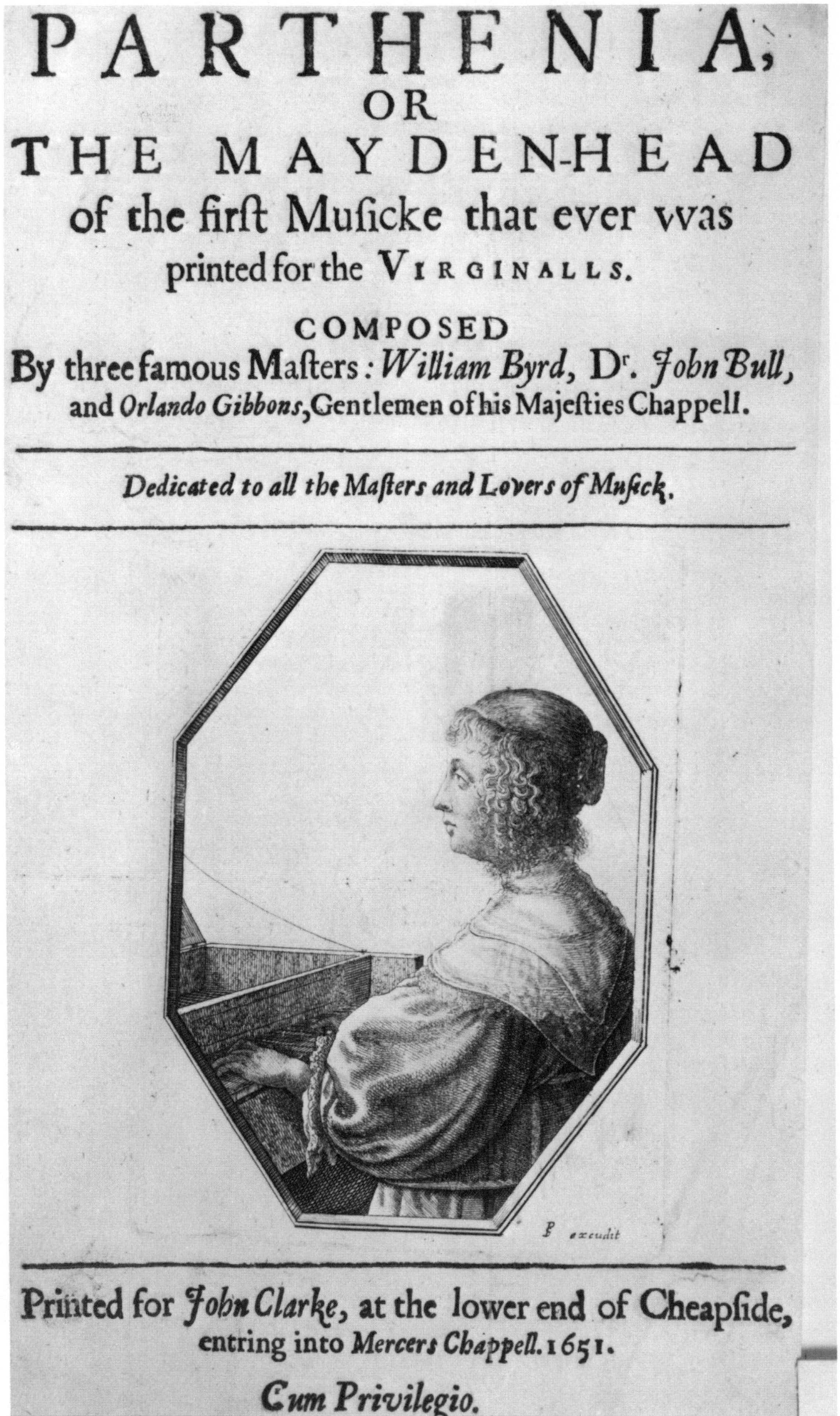

PARTHENIA,
OR
THE MAYDEN-HEAD
of the first Musicke that ever was
printed for the VIRGINALLS.

COMPOSED
By three famous Masters: *William Byrd*, Dr. *John Bull*,
and *Orlando Gibbons*, Gentlemen of his Majesties Chappell.

Dedicated to all the Masters and Lovers of Musick.

Printed for *John Clarke*, at the lower end of Cheapside,
entring into *Mercers Chappell*. 1651.

Cum Privilegio.

110. Title page for *Parthenia, or The Maidenhead* (1651). P. 1735.

A book of music for the virginal (hence the pun in the title), it contained music by William Byrd, John Bull and Orlando Gibbons. The title page of the original 1611 edition showed a lady of considerably less sensitivity touching the keys. The lady here is possibly a portrait of Hollar's wife.

111. Large map of England with inset town plans, including London afire. P. 648 (reduced 40%).

This print evidently dates from between 1666 and 1670.

A MAP OF BOTH CITTIES LONDON AND WESTMINSTER, BEFORE THE FIRE.
A. The Citty of London, B. The Citty of Westminster; C. Suburbes of London, D. Liberties of Westminster,
1 White Hall
2 S. Iames
3 the Parke,
4 S. Iames Fields,
5 Coventgarden
6 S. Martins Fields,
7 S. Giles Fields
8 Lincolns Inn Fields
9 Grayes Inn Fields
10 Smith Field
11 Moore Fields
12 Spittle Fields
13 Artilery ground
14 Clarendon house
15 Southampton house
16 Charingcrosse
17 Westminster Abby
18 S. Paul in London
19 Parliament house
20 Westminster Staires
21 Whitehall Staires
22 Lambeth ferry
23 Charingcrosse Staires
24 Strand bridge
25 Temple Staires
26 Black Friars Staires
27 Queene Hythe
28 Belins gate
29 Custome House
30 Tower wharfe
31 The Tower
32 Towerhill
33 S. Catharins
34 The Bridge
35 White Chapell Styl
36 Bishopsgate Street
Southwarke
Lambeth
PROSPECT OF THE CITTY OF LONDON, AS IT APPEARED, IN THE TIME OF ITS FLAMES.
Southwarke
On the 2 of September in ye Yeare 1666 (being the Lords day) in the morning, there hapned a dreadfull Fire, in ye house of one Mr Farmer a Baker in pudding lane, which Continued till about 3 at night the Wednesday following, in which time it burnt 89 Churches, thirteene thousand & two hundred houses, 636 acres, of 97 Parishes within ye Walls, there was but 11 left intire,
One Robert Hubert of Roane in Normandy, upon examination, Confessed he was one that fired the first house (viz) Mr Farmers in Pudding lane, for which fact he was Shortlie after hanged at Tiburne,
The Iles of Orkney
THE NORTH SEA
THE IRISH SEA
THE GERMANE OCEAN
A great Victory obtained by the English against ye Dutch June 3. 1665.
THE BRITISH OR NARROW SEA
The Ile of Wight
INFERIOR
GERMANIE
PART OF
FRANCE
Zeelandia
Yorke
Warwick
Southwark

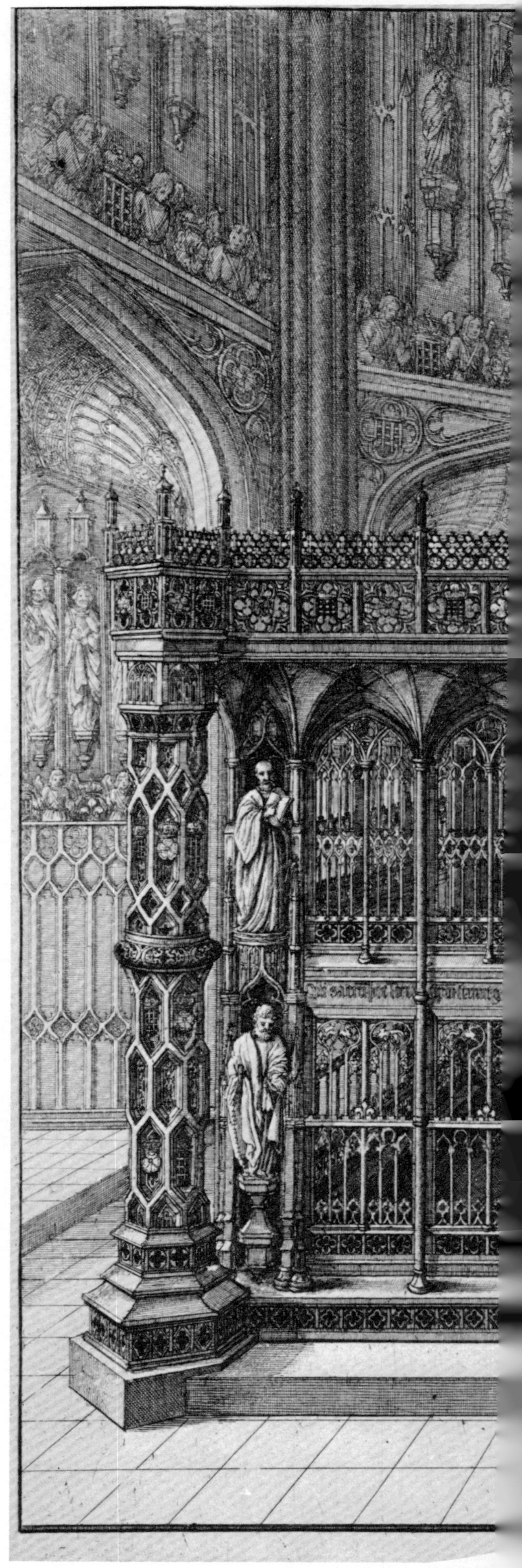

112. Henry VII's tomb in Westminster Abbey, from Sandford's *Genealogical History of the Kings of England* (1677). P. 2303 (reduced 15%).

A plate of marvellous strength and delicacy in the rendering of detail.

dieu ... mercie
Reuerendissimo in Christo Patri,
GILBERTO Diuina Providentia
ARCHIEPISCOPO CANTVARIENSI,
totius Angliæ PRIMATI, et Metropolitano,
nec non Serenissimi Dni. Regis CAROLI
IIdi e Sanctioribus Consilijs.
Hanc Sacelli figuram, in quo Rex HENRICVS, ejus nominis VII.mus jacet Tumulatus,
cum Prospectu partis Regis ejusdem Capellæ,
H. D. D. D. F. S.
W: Hollar fecit, aqua forti. A° 1665. Ætat: 58. compl:

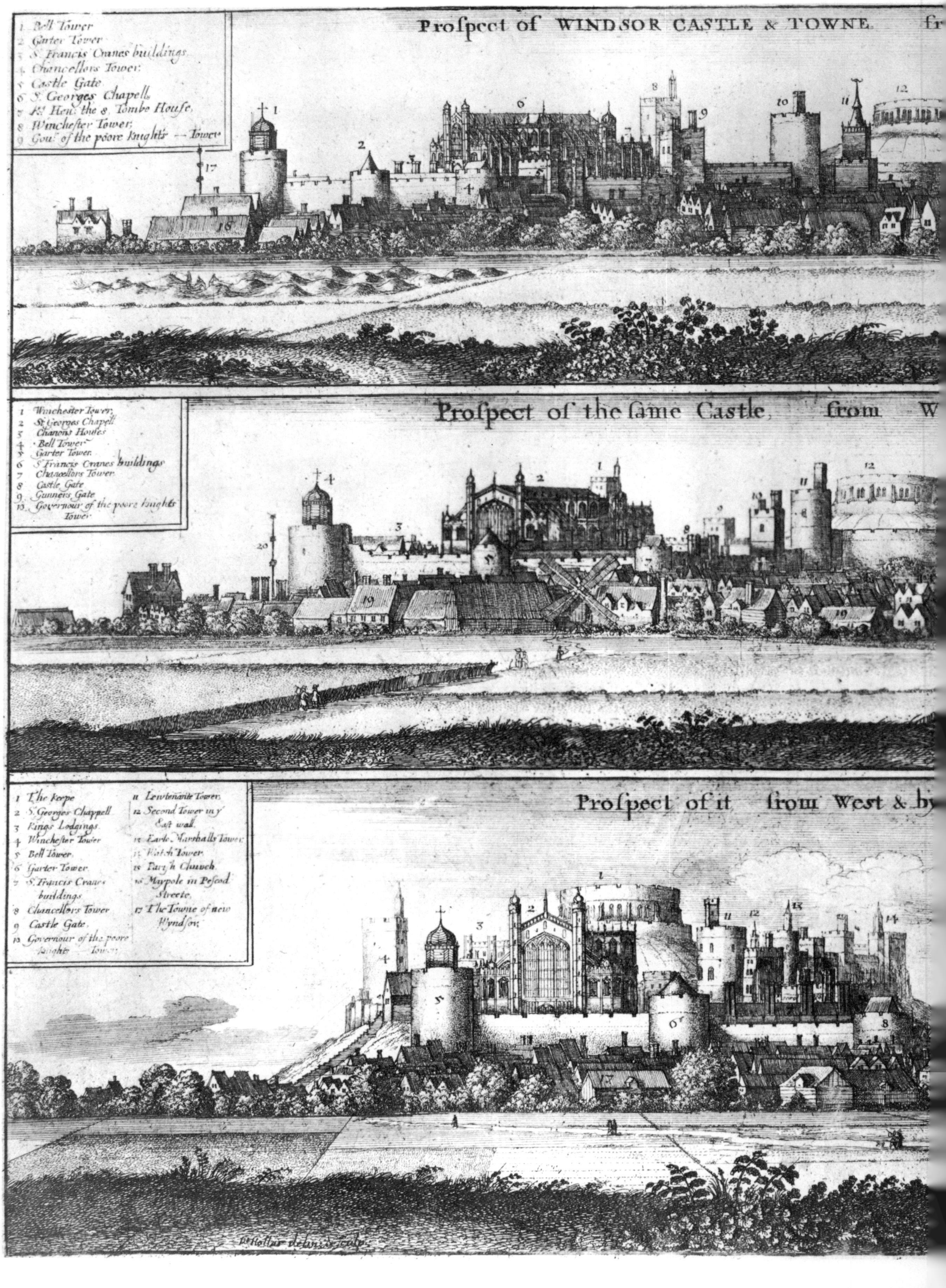
Prospect of WINDSOR CASTLE & TOWNE
1 Bell Tower
2 Garter Tower
3 Sr Francis Cranes buildings
4 Chancellors Tower
5 Castle Gate
6 S. Georges Chapell
7 Kg Hen: the 8 Tombe House
8 Winchester Tower
9 Gour of the poore Knights — Tower
Prospect of the same Castle, from
1 Winchester Tower
2 St Georges Chapell
3 Chanons Houses
4 Bell Tower
5 Garter Tower
6 Sr Francis Cranes buildings
7 Chancellors Tower
8 Castle Gate
9 Gunners Gate
10 Governour of the poore knights Tower
Prospect of it from West &
1 The Keepe
2 S. Georges Chappell
3 Kings Lodgings
4 Winchester Tower
5 Bell Tower
6 Garter Tower
7 S. Francis Cranes buildings
8 Chancellors Tower
9 Castle Gate
10 Governour of the poore knights Tower
11 Lewtenants Tower
12 Second Tower in ye East wall
13 Earle Marshalls Tower
14 Watch Tower
15 Parish Church
16 Maypole in Pescod Streete
17 The Towne of new Wyndsor

113. Three views of Windsor, from Ashmole's *Order of the Garter* (1672). P. 1073.

114. Windsor Castle, south side.
P. 658 (reduced 5%).

The fine figures wearing the robes of the Order of the Garter effectively demonstrate Hollar's sense of the dramatic properties of costume. This picture (of 1666) stands as the headpiece over the county map in Ashmole's *Antiquities of Berkshire*, which was belatedly published in 1719.

115. Windsor Castle, from the north; from Ashmole's *Order of the Garter* (1672). P. 1074 (reduced 10%).

The surprising feature of this plate is the acknowledgement at the bottom that it is after a drawing by Sir Christopher Wren: one feels that the waterside range of buildings with their inhabitants is distinctively by Hollar. Perhaps this was originally an architectural drawing of Windsor by Wren that Hollar transformed into one of his characteristic scenes.

The barge appears to be carrying timber, more of which can be seen stacked up at the right of the picture.

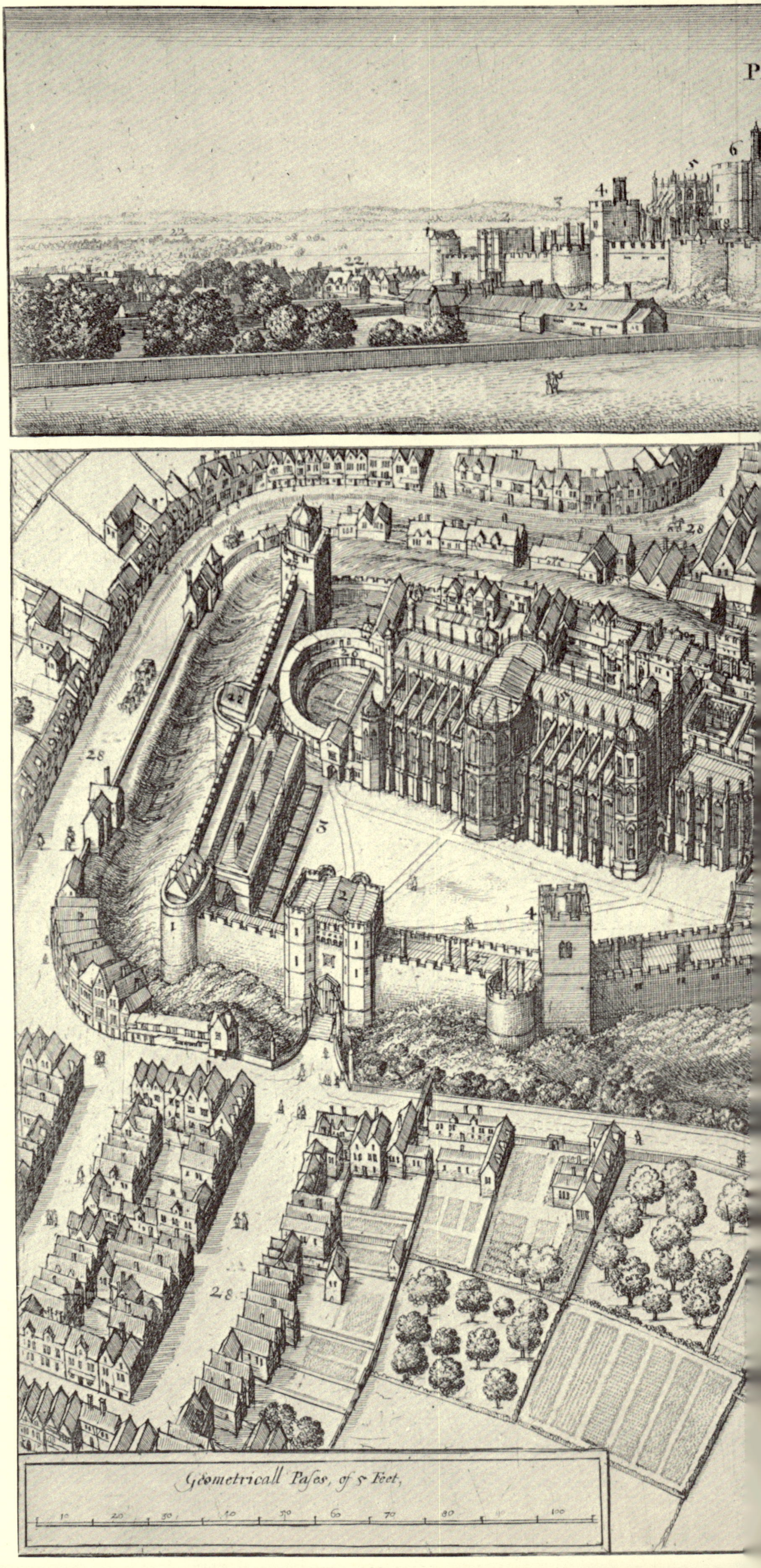

116. Bird's-eye view of Windsor, from Ashmole's *Order of the Garter* (1672). P. 1072.

A *tour de force* of aerial perspective.

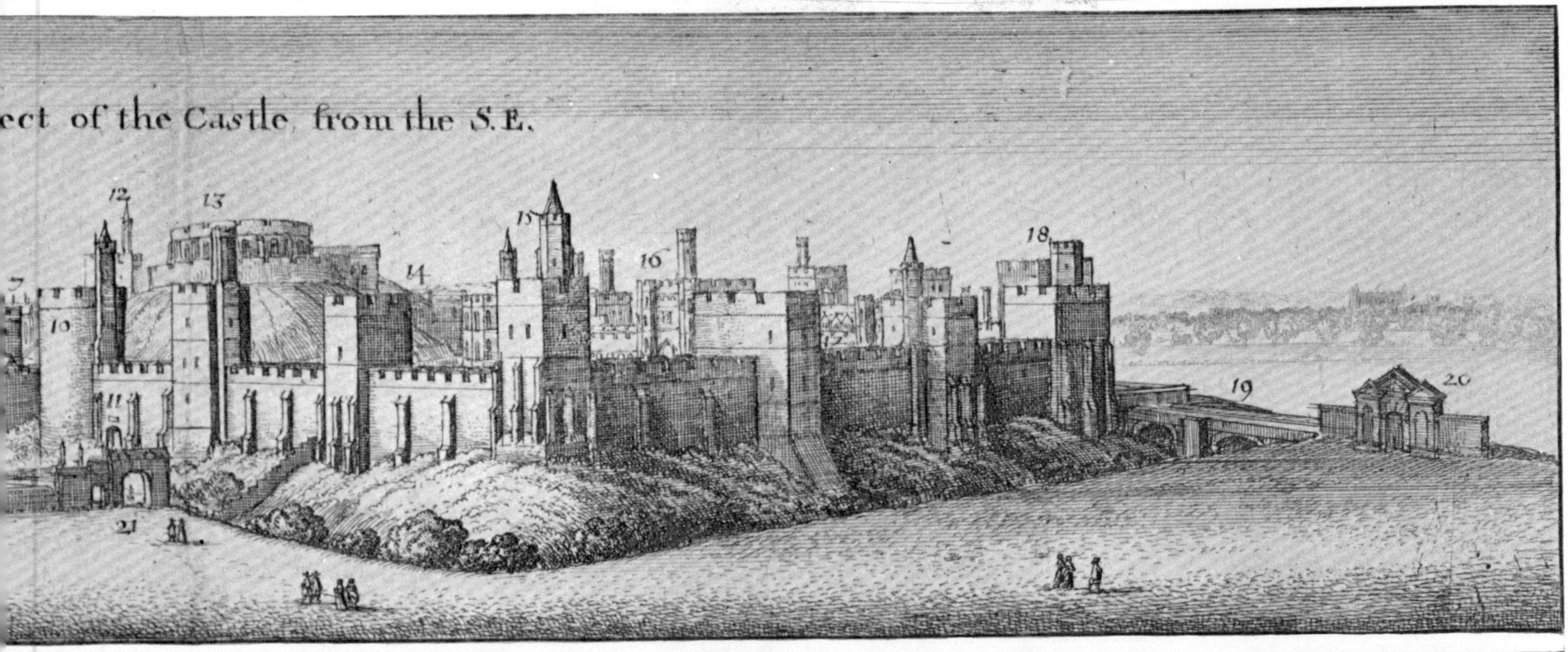
ect of the Castle, from the S.E.

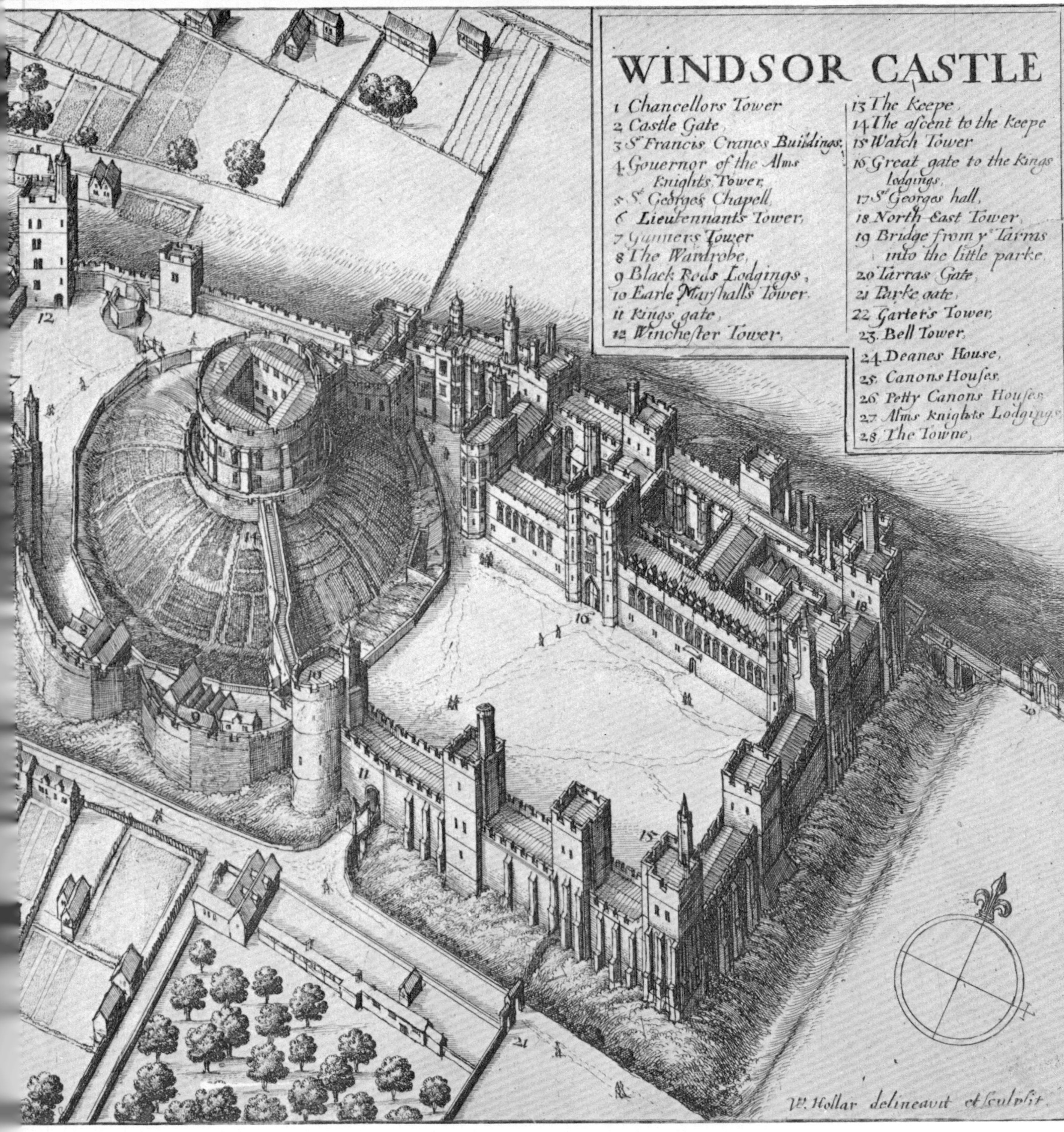
WINDSOR CASTLE
1 Chancellors Tower
2 Castle Gate,
3 Sr. Francis Cranes Buildings,
4 Gouernor of the Alms Knights Tower,
5 St. Georges Chapell,
6 Lieutennants Tower,
7 Gunners Tower
8 The Wardrobe,
9 Black Reds Lodgings,
10 Earle Marshalls Tower,
11 Kings gate,
12 Winchester Tower,
13 The Keepe
14 The ascent to the Keepe
15 Watch Tower
16 Great gate to the Kings lodgings,
17 St. Georges hall,
18 North East Tower,
19 Bridge from ye Tarras into the little parke,
20 Tarras Gate,
21 Parke gate,
22 Garter's Tower,
23 Bell Tower,
24 Deanes House,
25 Canons Houses,
26 Petty Canons Houses,
27 Alms Knights Lodgings,
28 The Towne,
W. Hollar delineavit et sculpsit.

117. A state banquet in St. George's Hall, Windsor Castle, from Ashmole's *Order of the Garter* (1672). P. 581.

The Knights of the Order are seen feasting in full regalia in a long line on the left of the table, whilst wave after wave of stewards bear dishes to them on the right. Charles II appears to be dining in solitary state at his private table.

Note the throng of onlookers in the foreground. Well-connected men like Pepys and Evelyn were often privileged to witness the junketings of the aristocracy at close quarters, but the file of pikes reminds one that certain lines were not to be crossed.
Evelyn describes a Garter Feast:
'The King sate on an elevated Throne at the upper end, at a table alone; the Knights at a table on the right hand reaching all the length of the roome; over against them a cuppord of rich gilded Plate etc; at lowere end the Musick; on the balusters above Wind musique, Trumpets and kettle drumms; the King was served by the Lords and pensioners, who brought up the dishes; about the middle of the dinner, the Knights drank the King's health, the King theirs; then the trumpets, musique etc plaied and sounded, the Gunns going off at the Tower; At the banquet came in the Queene and stood by the King's left hand, but did not sit; Then was the banqueting Stuff flung about the roome profusely; in truth the crowd was so greate, that though I staied all the supper the day before, I now staied no longer than this sport began for feare of disorder; The Cheer was extraordinary, each knight having 40 dishes to his messe, piled up 5 or 6 high; the roome hung with the richest Tapissry in the World.' (*Diary*, 23 April 1661.)

118. Ceremonial procession of the Knights of the Garter, from Ashmole's *Order of the Garter* (1672). P. 582.

A display of silken magnificence that must have reassured the readers of Ashmole's book that the aristocracy was safe in the full possession of its privileges after the years of deprivation and exile under the Commonwealth.

W: Hollar delineavit et sculpsit Aqua forti, 1672

119. Medallion of the insignia of the Order of the Garter, from Ashmole's *Order of the Garter* (1672). From P. 2620.

One of the five meticulous etchings from this plate: St. George slaying the dragon.

120 (right). St. George's Chapel, Windsor: the choir, looking west; from Ashmole's *Order of the Garter* (1672). P. 1079.

3. Arch over King Edw: 4. Tombe 5. Great Organ, 7. Roof of the Nave,
4. Choire dore, 6 Roof of the Choire, 8 West Window of the Chapel.

W. Hollar Scenographus Regis
delineavit et sculpsit.

121. Edward IV's tomb at Windsor, from Sandford's *Genealogical History of the Kings of England* (1677). P. 2282 (reduced 30%).

Parthey believed this to be Hollar's last work.

Bibliography

Aubrey, John. *Aubrey's Brief Lives,* ed. Oliver Lawson Dick. London, 1950.

Borovsky, F. A. *Wenzel Hollar. Nachträge zu Partheys Katalog.* Prague, 1898.

Cook, G. H. *Old S. Paul's Cathedral.* London, 1955.

Corbett, M. and R. W. Lightbown. *The Comely Frontispiece.* London, 1978.

Croft-Murray, E. and P. Hulton. *The British Museum Catalogue of British Drawings,* vol. I, *16th and 17th Centuries.* London, 1960.

Dostal, Eugen. *Wenceslaus Hollar.* Prague, 1924.

Evans, J. W. *Rudolph II and his World.* Oxford, 1973.

Evelyn, John. 'Sculptura: or The History and Art of Chalcography and Engraving in Copper', *Evelyn's Miscellaneous Writings.* London, 1825.

— *Diary,* ed. E. S. de Beer. Oxford, 1955.

— *Correspondence and Private Papers of John Evelyn,* ed. J. R. Tanner. London, 1926.

Fagan, L. *A Descriptive Catalogue of the Engraved Works of William Faithorne.* London, 1888.

Grossman, F. G. *Wenceslaus Hollar. 1607–1677. Drawings, Paintings and Etchings.* Manchester, 1963.

Haden, F. S. *About Etching.* London, 1879.

Hake, Henry M. 'Some Contemporary Records Relating to Francis Place', *Walpole Society,* vol. x.

Hamper, W. *The Life, Diary and Correspondence of Sir William Dugdale.* London, 1827.

Hervey, F. S. *The Life, Correspondence and Collections of Thomas Howard, Earl of Arundel.* Cambridge, 1921.

Hind, A. M. *Wenceslaus Hollar and his Views of London and Windsor in the 17th Century.* London, 1922.

— 'Wenceslaus Hollar', *Connoisseur,* XCII (Oct. 1933), pp. 215–27.

— *A History of Engraving and Etching.* New York, 1963 (reprint).

Hodges, C. Walter. *Shakespeare's Second Globe.* London, 1973.

Hodnett, Edward. *Francis Barlow.* London, 1978.

Hooke, Robert. *The Diary of Robert Hooke, 1672–80,* ed. Henry W. Robinson and Walter Adam. London, 1935.

Hulton, P. H. 'Drawings of England in the 17th Century by William Shellinks, Jacob Esselens and Lambert Doomer', *Walpole Society,* vol. XXXV.

Johnson, A.F. *A Catalogue of Engraved and Etched Title Pages.* Oxford, 1934.

Josten, C. H. (ed.). *Elias Ashmole (1617–1692).* Oxford, 1966.

Kratochvíl, Milos V. *Hollar's Journey on the Rhine.* Prague, 1965.

Martin, Margery. 'Wenceslaus Hollar and the British Antiquaries', *Motif,* 4 (1960), pp. 68–81.

Ogden, H. V. and M. S. *English Taste in Landscape in the 17th Century.* Ann Arbor, 1955.

Oppé, A. P. *English Drawings (Stuart and Georgian Periods) at Windsor Castle.* London, 1950.

Parry, Graham. 'Wenceslaus Hollar, The Antiquarians' Illustrator', in *Ariel,* April 1972.

— *Wenceslaus Hollar in England: A Tercentenary Exhibition.* Ashmolean Museum, Oxford, 1977.

— 'A New View of Bankside', in *Shakespeare Survey* 31. Cambridge, 1978.

Parthey, Gustav. *Wenzel Hollar. Beschreibendes Verzeichniss seiner Kupferstiche.* Amsterdam, 1963 (reprint).

Pav, J. I. 'Wenceslaus Hollar in Germany, 1627–36', *Art Bulletin* lv, 1973.

Pepys, Samuel. *The Diary of Samuel Pepys,* ed. Robert Latham and W. Matthews. London, 1970–7.

Powell, Anthony. *John Aubrey and his Friends.* London, 1948.

Rostenberg, Leona. *English Publishers in the Graphic Arts. 1599–1700.* New York, 1963.

Springell, Francis. *Connoisseur and Diplomat. The Earl of Arundel's Embassy to Germany in 1636.* London, 1963.

Sprinzels, F. *Hollar Handzeichnungen.* Vienna, 1938.

Tyler, R. *Francis Place 1647–1728.* York, 1971.

Urzidil, Johannes. *Wenzel Hollar, Der Kupferstecher Des Barock.* Vienna, 1936.

— *Hollar: A Czech Emigré in England.* London, 1942.

Van Eerde, Katherine. *Wenceslaus Hollar: Delineator of his Time.* Charlottesville, 1970.

Vertue, George. *A Description of the Works of the Ingenious Delineator and Engraver Wenceslaus Hollar, with some Account of his Life*. London, 1745.

Walpole, Horace. *A Catalogue of Engravers*. Strawberry Hill, 1763.

— *Anecdotes of Painting in England, with additions by Rev. J. Dallaway*. London, 1824; 1876.

Wheatley, Henry B. and Peter Cunningham. *London Past and Present*. London, 1891.

Whinney, Margaret and Oliver Millar. *English Art. 1625–1714*. Oxford, 1957.

Hollar etched the title pages and provided illustrations for a considerable number of books during his career. The following is a list of books printed in England which contain examples of his work.

Aesop. *Fables,* trans. J. Ogilby. 1665.
Allen, T. *A Chaine of Scripture Chronology*. 1659.
Allestree, R. *The Whole Duty of Man*. 1649.
Ambrose, I. *Prima et Ultima* (*First and Last Things*). 1659.
Andrewes, L. *The Form and Consecration of a Church*. 1659.
— *A Manual of Directions*. 1642.
Ashmole, E. *The Antiquities of Berkshire*. 1719.
— *The Institution of the Most Noble Order of the Garter*. 1672.
Barlow, F. *Severall Wayes of Hunting, Hawking and Fishing*. 1671.
— *Variae Quadrupedum Species*. 1662.
Biblia Polyglotta, ed. B. Walton. 1656.
Bibliotheca Regia or the Royal Library. 1659.
Blome, R. *Britannia*. 1673.
Brightman, T. *The Revelation of St. John Illustrated*. 1644.
Burton, William. *A Commentary on Antoninus his Itinerary*. 1658.
Cave, W. *Antiquitates Christianae*. 1675.
Cosin, D. *A Scholastical History*. 1657.
Diodati, J. *Pious Annotations upon the Holy Bible*. 1643.
Donne, J. *Biathanatos*. 1648.
Drexelius, J. *The Christians Zodiake*. 1643.
Dugdale, W. *The Antiquities of Warwickshire*. 1656.
— *A History of Embanking*. 1662.
— *The History of St. Paul's Cathedral*. 1658.
— *Monasticon Anglicanum*. Vol. I, 1655; vol. II, 1661; vol. III, 1673.
— *Origines Juridicales*. 1666.
Finch, H., Earl of Winchelsea. *The True Designe of the Late Eruption of Mount Aetna*. 1669.
Fuller, T. *The Church-History of Britain*. 1655.
— *Sermons*. 1658.
Hales, J. *Golden Remains*. 1659.
Hollar, W. *Animalium ferarum et bestiarum, florum, fructum . . Icones variae omnes ad vivum delineatae*. 1663.
— *Amoenissimae aliquot locorum prospectus*. 1644.
— *Aula Veneris sive varietas foeminini sexus*. 1644.
— *A Book of Drawings*. 1650.
— *Divers Anticke Faces after Leonardo da Vinci*. 1660.
— *Divers Views after the Life*. n.d.
— *Emblemata Nova*. n.d.
— *A New Book of Flowers and Fishes*. 1662.
— *Ornatus Muliebris Anglicanus*. 1640.
— *Theatrum Mulierum*. 1643.
Hammond, H. *A Practical Catechisme*. 1646.
Howell, J. *Instructions for Forraine Travell*. 1642.
— *Londinopolis*. 1657.
Homer. *Iliad*, trans. J. Ogilby. 1660.
Johnson, J. *Academy of Love*. 1641.
Jones, I. *Most Notable Antiquity of Great Britain, or Stone-Heng Restor'd*. 1655.
Juvenal. *Satires*, trans. R. Stapleton. 1660.
King, D. *The Cathedral Churches of England*. 1656.
Lovelace, R. *Lucasta*. 1659.
Lucretius, trans. J. Evelyn. 1656.
Manilius. *The Sphere*, trans. E. Sherburne. 1677.
Manual of Prayers and Litanies. n.d.
Martial. *Opera*. 1656.
Musaeum Tradescantianum. 1656.
Nieuhof, J. *An Embassy Sent by the East India Company to China*, trans. J. Ogilby. 1673.
Ogilby, J. *Africa*. 1670.
— *Britannia*. 1675.
— *The Entertainment of . . . Charles II*. 1661.
— *The Ephesian Matron*. 1666.
Paine, J. *Clidamas*. 1639.
Philpott, J. *Kent Surveyed*. 1659.
Psalmes of David, trans. M. Smith. 1668.
Sandford, F. *Genealogical History of the Kings of England*. 1677.
Sprat, T. *The History of the Royal Society*. 1667.
Talon, N. *The Holy History*. 1653.
Thoroton, R. *The Antiquities of Nottinghamshire*. 1677.
Upton, N. *De Studio Militari*. 1654.
Vicars, J. *Decapla in Psalmos*. 1639.
— *All the Memorable Parlamentary Mercies*. 1642.
Virgil, trans. J. Ogilby. 1674.
— ed. J. Ogilby. 1663.
Walker, W. *A New Dictionary of English Particles*. 1668.
Ware, J. *De Hibernia*. 1654.
— *Hibernia Antiqua*. 1658.
Whitlock, R. *Zootomia*. 1653.

Index

References from the Plate Section (numbered by illustration) are cited in bold type